Show Of

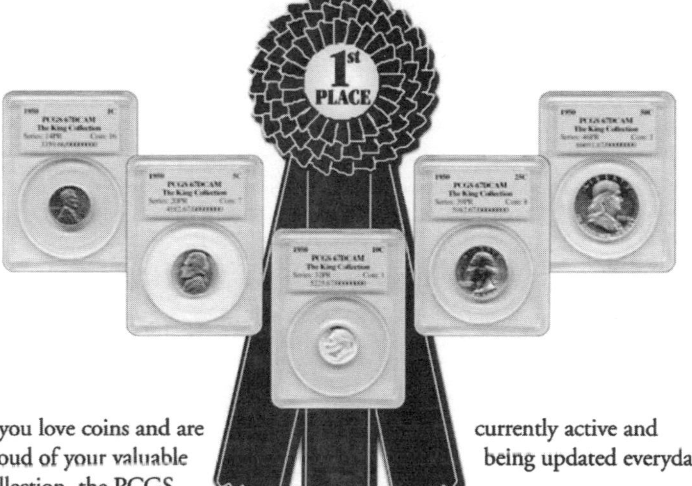

If you love coins and are proud of your valuable collection, the PCGS SET REGISTRY℠ is the perfect place to show off the results of your hard work. The Registry provides a safe place on the Internet to list your coins, graded by PCGS which is the largest and most respected coin grading service in the industry.

The PCGS SET REGISTRY℠ displays sets by type, denomination, series, and complete sets. You can compete with the some of the finest sets ever assembled by renowned collectors such as Eliasberg, Bass, and Price. Or, go head-to-head with over 10,000 awe-inspiring sets, which are currently active and being updated everyday.

The PCGS SET REGISTRY℠ is FUN! Registration is FREE and there are absolutely no fees to participate. Adding coins is as easy as typing in the certification number which appears on the PCGS insert. Simply go to www.pcgs.com and click on the Set Registry link. You can get instant gratification by seeing your collection displayed on the PCGS website.

Join the numismatic community, which has grown around the PCGS SET REGISTRY℠ and experience first hand why thousands collectors find the Registry a perfect place to show off their coins!

*Visit **www.pcgs.com** • email **setregistry@collectors.com** or call **800-447-8848***

A Division of Collectors Universe
NASDAQ: CLCT

Charles D. Daughtrey

Looking Through Lincoln Cents

Chronology of a Series - 2nd Edition

by

Charles D. Daughtrey

Copyright © 2005
Charles D. Daughtrey

cd@coppercoins.com
http://www.coppercoins.com
P.O. Box 6103, Springfield, MO 65801

Edited by Bob Piazza and Evangelia Daughtrey.
Contributing editor, Michael S. Keane

Photography by Charles D. Daughtrey, Bob Piazza, Billy Crawford, Richard S. Cooper, Garry M. Naples. Other photos from the Stewart Blay collection.

PUBLISHED BY

Zyrus Press, Inc.

PO Box 17810, Irvine, CA 92623
Tel: (888) 622-7823 / Fax: (800) 215-9694
www.zyruspress.com

ISBN # 0-9742371-4-0 (spiral)

DEDICATION

To my son Michael and my wife Evangelia, and the countless hours of patience they have had with me over the years while I studied Lincoln cents. Sagapaw, mecri ton ourano kai pio panw.

To my mother Connie and my father Mike, who taught me that being honest with others and myself is the most important virtue in life. Without honesty and integrity a person's life is a house of cards waiting to fall.

Words cannot adequately express the deep appreciation I have for your help and support through the years.

ACKNOWLEDGEMENTS

When I started coppercoins.com back in 1999, I was not prepared for the amount of support I was in store to receive on that and other numismatic projects. There have been countless offers for help by a large number of people, and to each of you I owe a debt of gratitude.

Special acknowledgement on this project goes out to Bob Piazza and Richard S. Cooper, whose collections and photography skills were openly volunteered to me, as they have been throughout my experience with these guys. Another special thanks to Doug Yost, who came through with one of the nicest RPM collections I have ever had the chance to see. You guys have really thick skin to put up with me, and I appreciate that.

There are too many others to whom I owe thanks in general for sending a coin or two, or for sending information my way, but I do want to especially thank a small group of people who have been there for me from the start:

Frank Baumann	Springfield Rare Coins
Billy Crawford	Craig Warren
Robert W. Frye	R. Williams
Jim Hiironen	Jack Sellards
Steve McKinnon	Robert Wilharm
Garry Naples	Roger Anderson
Gene Nichols	Ron Howard
Gary Wagnon	Gabriel Alonso

TABLE OF CONTENTS

CHAPTER 9:

FOREWORD

There's little doubt that the lowly cent is the most collected of United States coinage. It seems that just about everyone, at one time or another, has either bought or has been given a folder to store these coins. Those who are more than casual collectors, however, look for much more than just the date in these small copper coins. The Lincoln head cent, with both its classic Wheat and the current Memorial reverse, has had numerous design changes over time. In addition, there is a multitude of varieties and errors for this series, making it more collectible than ever.

As an avid collector for over 35 years, merely collecting these coins wasn't enough for me. Through a plastic magnifying glass I had accidentally discovered my first variety, a 1956-D repunched mintmark. The rest is history, as I now have over 1300 varieties in my personal collection.

The big question at the time for a novice collector such as myself was where could I get more information on these unique coins? Was there a comprehensive and updated listings of the many varieties out there? Where can I, at a glance, be able to attribute my coin? Was there a readily available source for this information? For

Bob Piazza, coppercoins.com senior numismatist.

those of you who do not already know, Mr. Chuck Daughtrey, a well-known and respected numismatic expert on the Lincoln cent, endeavored to fill this void.

With the advent of coppercoins.com in 1999, Chuck began the long, arduous task of documenting through microphotography and detailed analysis a complete listing of all known varieties for the Lincoln cent. Little did he realize that over 5 years later, he'd still be a far cry from realizing that dream. With over 1400 varieties and over 5000 photographs already on the site, there are still many more varieties waiting to be discovered. Newer varieties are being listed on a near-daily basis.

Looking Through Lincoln Cents does not address just varieties, but all things deemed important enough to annotate in one source book. It aims to keep the collector informed of the many aspects of collecting the Lincoln cent, and provides detailed, concise information in a chronological manner designed to both educated and entertain. To read this book is to discover what few people know about the Lincoln cent series — to see the Lincoln cent through Chuck's eyes and expertise.

I am sure you will enjoy the information contained herein. It has been a long time coming.

Bob Piazza, coppercoins senior numismatist

PREFACE

Over the past 15 years, I have been in contact with a number of collectors. Some of them provided me with answers, while others had many questions to ask. The most common question asked of me was, "What should I look for in X year cents?" The answer to this question cannot be easily summarized. I decided to write this book as a catchall, quick guide to the series that answers this question.

Although there are countless die varieties and anomalies in the Lincoln cent series that are not discussed within the pages of this publication, I intend to give enough of a general overview to serve as a good guide for those in search of answers. *Looking Through Lincoln Cents* shows a number of collectible die varieties, gives a report on the quality of cents produced each year, and shows a number of known minor anomalies for each year that are too common to be considered collectible errors or varieties.

Take note that this book is not an exhaustive attribution guide for all Lincoln cent die varieties. It is, rather, an attempt to provide a general overview of the series, year by year. For a more complete reference and attribution guide to individual die varieties, I suggest visiting my website at www.coppercoins.com.

Charles D. Daughtrey

INTRODUCTION

Pull a few pennies from your pocket. Take a close look. You may be holding an oddity that the United States Mint did not want you to find. Yet millions of them have found their way into general circulation. Many are worth hundreds of dollars. Experts call these anomalies "die varieties."

What is a die variety?

Throughout this book you will see microscopic images of coins that are collectible not only because of their date and place of mintage, but also because of an anomaly on the coin created by the design on the particular die from which they were minted. How is this possible? Every flaw, scratch, or mark placed onto a die transfers to the coins that it mints. By using magnification to examine the flaws and marks left behind on a coin from the dies, the coin can be matched to the dies that were used to create it. This process of identification is called "attributing," and the coins of interest that gained the die's fingerprints of flaws (usually doubling) during the process that made the die are called "die varieties."

This book has been painstakingly written to include not only some of the general information about this coin series in an easy to follow chronological format, but also to inform the reader of the anomalous coins minted each year that can bring profit to those who find them.

What makes a die variety valuable?

A die variety is valuable because it features design flaws that differ from a "normal" coin. In many cases, these design flaws are highly collectible, relatively scarce, and carry a significant and valuable premium.

Die varieties are not supposed to happen, but for one reason or another, they do. When a coin does escape the myriad of quality control procedures at the United States Mint (including hand inspecting each die with a microscope), astute coin dealers and hobbyists quickly snatch them up. The untold story, however, is that just as many slip into general circulation, destined to become mere pocket change.

These oddities of the minting process escape mint detection and are found by collectors with a scrutinizing eye. They are something different to collect — something that has a design that was not intended to appear as it does.

Since die varieties are far less common than coins that do not exhibit such flaws, they carry a premium value to collectors. The first part of a die variety's value comes from the same aspects that make any coin valuable — its age, mintage, and condition. Beyond those basic parts to any coin's value, die varieties warrant additional premium value because of their desirability as examples of a mint flaw. This includes their relative rarity to other die varieties as well as the amount of effort it takes to see the die variety. Those visible to the naked eye are generally worth more, as are those for which few examples have been found.

So why should I get this book?

In the past, no book completely addressed all the fascinating and collectible aspects of the Lincoln cent series. In part, this was because the market for buying and selling Lincoln cent die varieties was still in its infancy.

Today, the market has grown significantly, and the knowledge base of collectors has far outpaced the information available in any book on Lincoln cents.

For seven years not a single newly released book provided specific and comprehensive treatment to the Lincoln cent series. During those years much has happened that affects how cents are collected, but little has been published in an effort to inform the collector.

That's where this book comes in. Looking Through Lincoln cents provides a broad update and helps provide valuable information on the series long sought after by collectors and dealers.

Where are die varieties bought and sold?

The market for buying and selling die varieties is a growing subset of the overall coin collecting market. The Internet has significantly increased the general awareness of die varieties. While many collectors still collect strictly by denomination, type, or date, the number of collectors who at the very least want an example of a nice die variety in their collection is growing quickly. This fact lends greatly to the heavy increases in value for the most obvious die varieties. Most dealers will purchase the more obvious die varieties at a strong premium over the listed value of a normal coin for that reason.

The vast majority of die varieties are too minor for less specialized, or "generalist" collectors. These include collectors who want an example of a design and collect by type, or who want to complete a basic set of a given series by date and mint only. For most of these collectors, any die variety that takes more than five power magnification to see is considered "flyspeck" collecting and does not pique their interest.

The die variety market is specialized and may be difficult to find without guidance. Ebay®, a major online auction site located at www.ebay.com, is a major outlet for buying and selling die varieties. Yahoo® Auctions is another major source for die variety collectors. Usually found in the "errors" category under "U.S. Coins" on either site, specialized die variety collectors buy and sell die varieties regularly, often accompanied by microscopic images showing the anomalous characteristics that make the coin special. Caution must be exercised when purchasing at online auction sites because the coins being sold are often unchecked by knowledgeable students of the hobby and are not necessarily what they are advertised to be.

A more reliable resource for die variety collectors can be found by conducting an Internet search for dealers who specialize in die varieties. These dealers tend to offer coins that have been closely checked for authenticity and they stand to lose much more if their reputation is damaged by selling coins other than as advertised. Many times, these dealers are good points of contact to buy or sell die varieties.

Dealers who travel the trade show circuit promoting and selling die varieties are less common. In many cases the more significant die varieties can be found with little effort at shows, but the less obvious examples are generally left to collectors and online dealers. The most abundant source of die varieties at a trade show, however, can be found every January in Florida. The FUN (Florida United Numismatists) Show has become an annual mecca for the die variety market. Information regarding this show can be found at the FUN website, www.funtopics.com.

Who buys die varieties?

Most collectors begin their Lincoln cent collection by finding and purchasing quality specimens that comprise a "basic set." With time, these collectors begin looking for a new, more expansive way to collect without abandoning their chosen series. Die varieties provide a way for collectors to expand a series of a couple hundred coins into a new level of collecting, all within that same series. The Lincoln cent series, for example, contains fewer than 250 different coins for a "basic set" consisting of one example of each date and mintmark. A full variety set of Lincoln cents currently stands at over 2,000 different coins. Because examples of previously unknown dies are being found and cataloged all the time, the number of coins required for the full variety set is constantly growing.

Another small yet important reason for the growing die variety collector market is that collectors can gain notoriety in published works by submitting new die varieties to the authors. To date, many die varieties have not been catalogued. A collector who does find a new die variety can send his or her coin in for attribution and inclusion into the die cataloging system, and he or she will often receive a certificate or credit for finding the new die.

Where are die varieties found?

Surprisingly enough, die varieties are all around you, all the time. They may be difficult to locate and will take patience and effort, but they can be found in your pocket change, coin jars, and rolls or bags of coins purchased at face value from local banks. While most of the major and valuable die varieties have already been located and placed into the die variety market, nice examples of valuable die varieties are still regularly found for a mere fraction of their value.

Other sources include dealer stock at coin shops and shows. Many dealers do not have the time or patience to go through all the coins they buy and sell looking for microscopic anomalies. They often do not mind collectors "cherry picking" their stock for such coins. The dealers still make a profit by selling the coins, regardless of what the coins exhibit.

Another die variety source is in original uncirculated rolls or bags of older coins. Dealers sell bulk rolls or bags at a premium over face value. Still, this premium is less than the price of the coins if they were valued individually. Most memorial reverse Lincoln cent (1959-date) rolls trade for less than three times their face value ($1.50 or less per roll). Uncirculated wheat cent rolls from the 1940's are still affordable as well. Uncirculated rolls of coins that bear the same mintmark and that were rolled by either a major bank or a currency holding and transportation company, such as Brinks or Wells Fargo, are often referred to as "B.U. rolls." Any of these provide a good source for searching for die varieties.

The pages that follow will take you through a comprehensive approach to die varieties. Detailed photographs and descriptions allow you to see not only what is worth collecting, but also common striking errors that may not be worth collecting at all.

With *Looking Through Lincoln Cents*, it is now easier than ever to learn about the Lincoln cent series and its increasingly popular die varieties.

Do you still have those pennies in your hand? You could very well be holding a rare die variety and not know it.

Good Luck!

1 | THE DIE MAKING PROCESS

First and foremost, knowing what to look for on any coin for valuable doubling requires an understanding of how that coin was created. All forms of collectible doubling on coins occur during the die making process, before any coins are struck with the die. In other words, doubled dies and mintmark varieties actually occur before a single coined example is struck, because the doubling discussed is impressed into the die before the die is ever sent to the coining press.

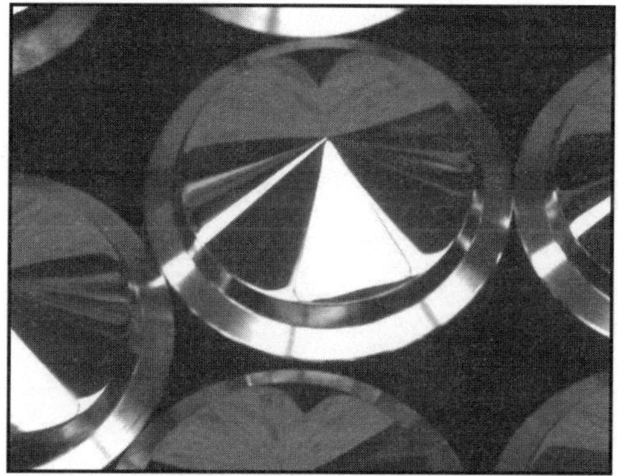

Blank coining dies sit in a box awaiting their turn at the hubbing press. Photo by Rich Schemmer.

Coining dies are a bar of steel impressed with a mirror-image impression of a coin design, called a negative relief. They are "hubbed" in a hubbing press, which is a machine that slowly impresses the design into the die. Prior to 1997, the hubbing press was pressed into coining dies up to eight times to completely fill out the recesses of the design. Between these hubbings, the die was hardened in an oven in preparation for another hubbing. It was between these hubbings that the possibility for doubling occurred.

Dies have slots called "keys" that ensure they are aligned properly in the hubbing and coining presses. If these keys are broken, damaged, or intentionally filed off (as was sometimes the case), it becomes nearly impossible to perfectly realign the die in the hubbing press. When the next hubbing occurs, the result is a doubling of the design.

Since this doubling is a part of the die that mints the coins, all coins minted with a given doubled die take on the doubling. With this in mind, all coins minted by a doubled die have the same characteristics of doubling, since a coin is an exact mirror-image impression of the die that created it. These coins can then be compared to one another and cataloged using a system of numbers to represent each die. Any coin struck by that die carries its die number.

Completely hubbed dies receive a full impression of the design. Until they are used, these dies are stored in a vault at the Mint. Until 1990, engravers at the Philadelphia Mint, where all dies were made, would use a small metal punch and mallet to hammer a mintmark into the die before sending that die to one of the branch mints (Denver or San Francisco).

Because the mintmark was applied by hand, minor mistakes often occurred. For example, punches bounced or mintmarks were applied slightly out of place and then corrected. These mistakes and corrections

Finished coining dies await their turn for use after inspection. The die with the "E" written onto it is defective and will be resurfaced and rehubbed before use. Photo by Rich Schemmer.

show on the coins as a "repunched mintmark," or RPM. Like with doubled dies, the doubling of the mintmark letter happened on the die before the die was placed into use on the coining press. Coins minted with these dies show the same characteristics as doubling and can be compared and given catalog numbers that correspond to the die that minted the coin.

On rare occasion, an incorrect mintmark would be placed on a die and then corrected to show the proper letter for the branch mint to which the die would be shipped for use. If the effort to remove the improper mintmark was not complete before punching the proper letter into the die, an "over mintmark," or OMM would result. OMMs are rare in occurrence and are not always easy to detect. In fact, OMMs are far less common than RPMs, which explains why they command a higher premium value.

Mention of specific dates has been made in the preceding paragraphs, because changes in technology and equipment at the Mint have affected the die making process, thus changing how die varieties happen, if they even do.

In 1990, the Mint abandoned punching mintmarks directly into the individual coining dies. Instead, the Mint opted to machine the mintmark directly into the master die, which is the primary design used to create all hubs and, indirectly, all dies made for the year. Because a machined letter replaced the hand punch, it became virtually impossible to create RPMs and OMMs. There are no known examples of these die varieties on cents past 1989.

In 1997, the Mint stopped production of dies using the multiple hubbing technique in favor of a faster and more efficient method in which dies were hubbed only once. This "single-squeeze" method of die making saved time and expense and lessened the chances of making mistakes such as doubled dies.

For years after this method was introduced, a number of numismatists believed it was impossible to create doubled dies, while others insisted they were still possible. Coins with doubling dated after 1996 have been found and explained as doubled dies by some, and as striking anomalies by others. The judgment as to whether these coins are actually doubled dies will ultimately rest with the individual collectors, but it is the opinion of the author of this book that the dies presented, which are not supposed to fit into the "doubled die box" because of their method of manufacture, are indeed doubled dies. How they were produced is a mystery. Their characteristics, however, are undeniably those of doubled dies.

2 | DOUBLED DIES EXPLAINED

Hub doubling, the cause of doubled dies, happens when the hub (positive image of the coin's design) or the die (the negative relief tool that makes the coins) shifts in position between impressions. Because this shift in position can happen in many different ways, experts and collectors use a classification system to describe the appearance of this shift to other collectors.

The categories of hub doubling are known as "classes." They are assigned strictly by appearance — regardless of the exact mechanism or step in the die making process that caused the doubling. To clarify, it doesn't matter if the doubling happened in the second, third, or last hubbing of a die. What does matter is the direction of spread and type of spread shown.

All doubled dies carry the attributes of at least one of nine different classes. A single class is used for doubled dies that can be accurately described using only one class. Two or more classes are used to describe doubling that happens in such a fashion that a single class would not suffice, or for dies that are tripled, quadrupled, and so on.

This section will show the nine classes of doubling and what makes them different from each another. It will also show the most common cases where classes must be put together to properly describe doubling found on coins. Finally, it will show some examples of doubling caused by mechanical error in the striking process that are not doubled dies at all.

Class 1 — Rotated Hub Doubling

Rotated hub doubling occurs when the die is turned either clockwise or counterclockwise on an axis near the center of the design between hubbings. It is characterized by having all devices nearer the rim doubled the most, while those nearer the center of the design are not doubled at all.

Class 1 hub doubling is somewhat scarce in the number of times it appears on different dies, but it happens to be the best known of all classes because of two famous doubled dies. 1955P-1DO-001, the famous "1955 doubled die," is class 1 hub doubling, as is its modern-day cousin, 1972P-1DO-001, or the famous "1972 doubled die."

The famous 1955 and 1972 doubled dies are both very classic cases of class 1 rotated hub doubling. Top photo by author, bottom photo by Bob Piazza.

There are a number of cases where class 1 hub doubling is apparent on the Lincoln cent, but the two dies just mentioned are the most famous. Other examples include 1939P-1DO-001, which received an early hubbing that was rotated drastically counterclockwise to the later hubbings that finished off the design. We know that it was an earlier hubbing that caused the doubling because only the central areas of the design are affected. Dies start out with a slight conical shape on their face and, as a result of this shape, the first hubbing (and often the second) only affects the central areas of the design.

Class 2 — Distorted Hub Doubling

Distorted hub doubling occurs when a hub flattens out between hubbings on a single die. This happens because the hubs are used to create a number of dies (often over a hundred). As with any mallable material, the steel flattens outward as it is used. If a die is first hubbed with a hub that is rather new and subsequently with an old hub, the devices near the outer edge will show doubling either toward the center of the design (flattened hub used first) or toward the edge of the design (flattened hub used last).

Class 2 hub doubling is most often characterized by doubling that parallels the outside edges of the devices closest to the rim. It sometimes shows all the way around the design and other times it does not. The two primary requirements are that the spread be directly toward or away from the rim (without rotation or pivot) and that there be clear separation lines in the doubling.

This class of doubling is also often combined with class 5 and class 6 hub doubling. See adding classes of doubling in the next section for more information.

Top: *Very well defined class 2 doubling shows on this example of 1964D-1DR-002.*

Bottom: *Much more minor class 2 doubling on an unattributed 1964-D cent. both photos by author.*

Class 3 — Design Hub Doubling

This class of hub doubling is one of the most interesting of all doubled dies. It is caused when two different hubs with different designs are used to create one die. The design differences can be as minor as the exact placement of a single letter or design feature, or it can be as major as two different dated hubs.

Because punching date digits into individual dies ended with nineteeth century coin types, ALL examples of what people refer to as "overdates" in twentieth century coin types are actually class 3 doubled dies. This includes the 1918/7-D nickel, both 1942/1 dimes, the 1943/2-P nickel, as well as others.

Design hub doubling is characterized by a difference in some part of the design rather than misalignment of the design. Thus, it can show on any part of the design and can take on many different appearances.

The 1960 proof cents hubbed with both large and small date hubs are the best known examples of such doubling in the Lincoln cent series. Likewise, the 1970-S proof die, hubbed with both large and small date hubs, is another very nice example.

1970S-1DO-003 is a classic example of a class 3 doubled die. This die was hubbed with a small date and large date hub. The difference is best noted in the 9 and 7 digits. Photo by author.

Class 4 — Offset Hub Doubling

Offset hub doubling is caused when a die is returned to the hubbing press and has a misalignment that is not rotated or pivoted in any fashion, but is rather shifted to one direction with otherwise proper alignment. The result is doubling of the design in a single cardinal direction — north, south, east, southwest, etc.

This form of doubling is found more often affecting the center of the design than other classes of doubling, because regardless of the strength of the offset, all devices, including those in the center of the design, will show the same spread of doubling. Class 4 doubling is unlike other types of doubling because, as a rule, most doubling affects the outer devices. Even in the case of pivoted and rotated hub doubling with strong spreads there is little evidence of doubling in the center of the design.

The best known cases of class 4 hub doubling in the Lincoln cent series include the 1942 doubled eye varieties, the major 1983 doubled die reverse, and the 1984 and 1997 doubled ear varieties. Many others exist, even though this is one of the least common types of hub doubling.

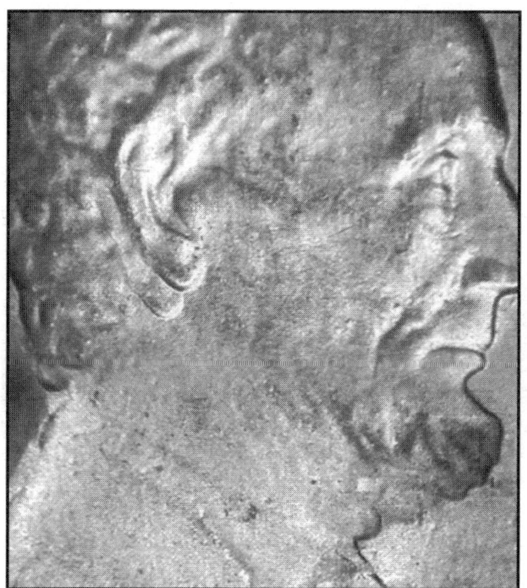

1984P-1DO-001 is one of the well known examples of offset hub doubling. Note the northeast spread on the earlobe, the beard, and on the bowtie. These are the only areas of the design affected because the offset occured in an early hubbing when the die still had its conical shape, thus only receiving the center of the design in the offset hubbing. Photo by Bob Piazza.

Class 5 — Pivoted Hub Doubling

This class of hub doubling is one of the more common types of doubling. Its cause is very close to that of class 1 rotated hub doubling in that the alignment of the die that created the doubling involves clockwise or counterclockwise rotation, but in the case of class 5 hub doubling, the center of rotation is at or near the rim, causing more doubling on one side of the design (the area opposite the pivot point), and little or no doubling near the pivot point.

This class of doubling shows a clockwise or counterclockwise spread that gets stronger toward one side of the design. There are many cases of this class of doubling in the Lincoln cent series, but by far the best known example is 1995P-1DO-001, a very strong, but rather common, doubled die.

It is common to hear the spread on class 5 doubled dies described using the position of digits on the face of a clock, with the four cardinal directions being 12, 3, 6, and 9. For sake of description, 1995P-1DO-001 is described as having a spread "from K-4," meaning that the central pivot point is at the rim near the 4 o'clock position, or just below the date. This is evident because the strongest doubling on the coin is around the word IN of the motto at about 10 o'clock, or K-10.

1995P-1DO-001 shows almost no doubling in the date, but shows strong doubling closer to the rim on LIBERTY and the first half of the motto. This is because the pivot point of the doubling is near the date. Photos by author.

Class 6 — Distended Hub Doubling

Class 6 doubled dies are in a league of their own: they represent the only class of doubled die that lacks clear separation in the doubling. They are generally caused by using hubs to impress designs into improperly annealed (heated) dies. The design flattens out and becomes stretched or distended toward the outside of the design. Like class 2 doubled dies, class 6 doubled dies generally show their characteristics close to the rim.

As a rule, class 6 doubled dies show thicker devices. The thickness is always more noticeable in the parts of the devices that are parallel to the rim and is not as noticeable on the areas of devices that are perpendicular to (point towards) the rim.

Some of the most notable class 6 doubled dies are found generally on the reverse of cents dating 1934-1944 and on the obverse of those dating 1937-1945. Why the Mint had such problems during this era is a mystery, but it seems (from the lack of dies known) that the problem was corrected around 1946. Examples of class 6 doubled dies are known for all eras of the Lincoln cent, but they are far less in number than the periods stated above.

1944D-1DO-001 shows a very nice classic example of distended hub doubling. Note the stretching toward the rim and how the device areas pointing toward the rim are nearly normal while those parallel to the rim are extemely thick. Photo by Author.

Class 7 — Modified Hub Doubling

This class of doubling is caused when an errant part of a design is ground off a hub in an effort to replace it. If the errant portion of the design is not completely removed by the grinding it will leave its mark on any die created from that hub. The errant element is usually a digit or digits of the date, but it can be other parts of the design.

Compared to other classes of doubling, there are relatively few class 7 doubled dies in the Lincoln cent series. The best-known example is 1963D-1DO-001, which shows a very low 3 digit that was partially ground off and replaced with a normal 3 digit. Other examples include 1970-minted cents that have portions of ground off date digits remaining on the dies.

The main distinguishing characteristic of class 7 doubled dies — as opposed to other classes of doubling with one digit out of place — is that the doubled digit is generally soft and weak. For class 7 doubling, this weakness results from the polishing or grinding away of that digit on the hub. Many of the doubled dies with single digits or letters near the rim that are slightly out of place can be described more accurately using other classes. See class 8 for further explanation.

1963D-1DO-001 is the best known example of class 7 hub doubling. Photo by author.

Class 8 — Tilted Hub Doubling

Tilted hub doubling occurs when a die is set in the hubbing press out of flush and rotated clockwise or counterclockwise from the hub. The resulting doubled die will show doubling on part of the design close to the rim, and the rest of the design will be normal. In addition to the partial design left behind by the tilted hubbing, the die and hub are generally flat, causing the doubling to show signs of weakness in the central focus before disappearing around the rim in either direction.

The best-known example of class 8 hub doubling is one of the first dies assigned with this class back in the early 1990s. At that time class 8 was deemed necessary as an addition to the seven known classes, which had been the standard for a long time. This die, 1964P-1DO-002, shows a counterclockwise spread only on the L of LIBERTY and the word IN of the motto. The die was placed in the hubbing press tilted to the right as you view the coin. As a result, the doubling only shows on the left side of the design.

A large number of other examples of this class of hub doubling have been assigned, most having to do with a bar of doubling above or below the L of LIBERTY. These tend to be most common from 1961 to 1964, with dozens of different dies known for this period. Oddly enough, class 8 doubled dies are quite sparse in number compared to other classes of doubling in the Lincoln cent series.

1964P-1DO-002 shows classic tilted hub doubling. Photos by author.

Class 9 — Shifted Hub Doubling

The first class to be added to hub doubling in over ten years, shifted hub doubling, was adopted by researcher Billy Crawford as an explanation of how hub doubling can happen within a single hubbing of a die, most notably those created with the single squeeze hubbing technique adopted by the Mint in 1997. This form of doubling happens when a slightly misaligned die "pops" into position under the constant pressure of the hub and its thousands of pounds of force.

Probably the best analogy to use is a tire shop. If you have ever witnessed a new tire on a rim being filled with air for the first time, the pressure of the air pops the tire, often loudly, into place against the lip of the rim. Dies often make this same noise when being hubbed by a hubbing press.

This form of doubling is most often characterized by a slippage of the design, often the center devices, in a cardinal direction — much like class 4 offset hub doubling. The main difference is that the design is never "picked up" off the die during hubbing. Rather, it suddenly "slides" into place creating doubling in the design.

This class of doubling was added to the eight existing classes by most recognized sources (including coppercoins.com) in early 2004 after a number of recent minor doubled dies had been discovered and could not easily be explained using any of the existing classifications.

1994P-1DR-002, shows "wavy steps," a term given by collectors to the most common form of class 9 doubled dies. Photo by author.

Multiple Class Hub Doubling

Cases of hub doubling often surface that cannot be sufficiently explained with a single class. Sometimes these are because of hub tripling, and sometimes they are just oddities of classification that don't commonly happen. Either way, experts must come up with a method of describing these hubs that can be explained in simple terms.

Rather than devising new classifications for every case, experts have agreed to use multiple classes to explain these oddly formed doubled dies. When using more than one classification to describe a doubled die, note the class lowest in numerical order first, and then note any necessary additional classes in numerical order.

A doubled die that shows rotation and distortion would be described as a class 1 + 2 doubled die. Likewise, a doubled die that shows distortion and a pivot from a point near the rim would be described as a class 2 + 5 doubled die.

In rare cases, tripled or quadrupled dies exist that require as many as four different classes to describe the spread evident on different areas of the coin. Regardless of the placement and nature of the four different classes, always list them in ascending order.

For example, if a Lincoln cent obverse showed class 4 doubling to the southwest in the form of a doubled eyelid, class 3 doubling in LIBERTY, and class 2 + 5 doubling in the motto, the coin would still be described as a class 2 + 3 + 4 + 5, even though the class 2 and class 5 doubling are directly related.

To the novice at detecting and collecting doubled dies. all of this sounds like a different language. Do not despair — even though experts have thought out classes of doubling to a rough science, there is still a great deal of discrepancy in how they describe the same doubled die individually. The most important thing to remember is what the individual classes basically look like, and then not to give a die a classification that it could not possibly be. Anything else is generally acceptable.

There are two cases in the Lincoln cent series where using more than one classification to describe doubling becomes necessary far more often than in other cases. It is important to note, however, that an entire volume in itself could be written to comprehensively cover the subject.

The first case involves dies that exhibit doubling which is both distorted (class 2) and pivoted (class 5) in nature, creating the class 2 + 5 doubled die.

When a die receives a very slightly pivoted hubbing, it is usually unnoticeable except to the well trained eye. Once that pivoting is combined with distortion, the pivot is more visible because of the number of additional reference points provided by the distorted hubbing.

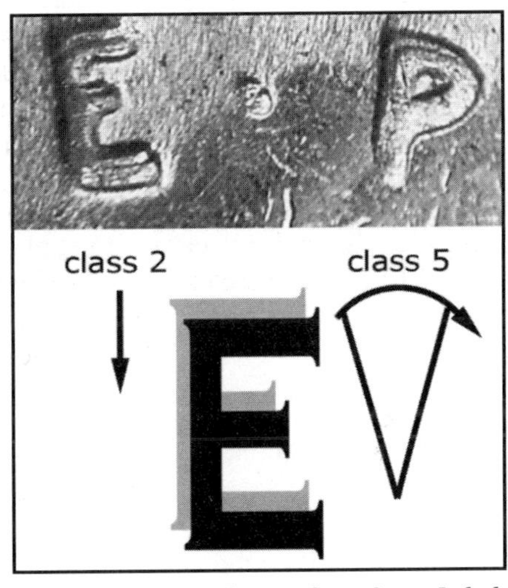

1946P-1DR-001 shows class 2 + 5 hub doubling. The class 2 spread is toward center and the class 5 spread is pivoted clockwise from the 9 o'clock position. Photo and illustration by author.

Since distorted hub doubling is described strictly as doubling that is either straight toward or away from the edge of the design, the pivot must be accounted for. The classification system puts the distorted hub doubling before the pivoted hub doubling in numerical order, or class 2 + 5.

The second common case of multiple class doubled dies in the Lincoln cent series involves those doubled dies, usually wheat cent reverse doubled dies, that show both distortion (class 2) and distention (class 6).

Because distorted hub doubling describes doubling with separation and distended hub doubling is by definition extra thickness, doubled dies that show both must be described using both classes.

These occur most frequently on wheat cent reverses in the bountiful class 6 years of 1934-1944. Some of the doubled dies from this period show separation lines, and by definition these cannot be described by using class 6 alone.

The example illustrated here is 1945P-1DR-005. It shows the clear separation of class 2 distorted hub doubling, but on the left side of the motto it also shows distention, or class 6 doubling as indicated by the stretched appearance of the overlapping letters. It would be described by using both class 2 and class 6, or class 2 + 6.

These two examples illustrate only the two most common multiple class doubled die styles for the Lincoln cent. Many different combinations of hub doubling have been encountered on Lincoln cents, but most are rather scarce. While developing a knack for attributing coins may seem difficult at first, any collector can learn this skill through practice and by carefully studying this reference.

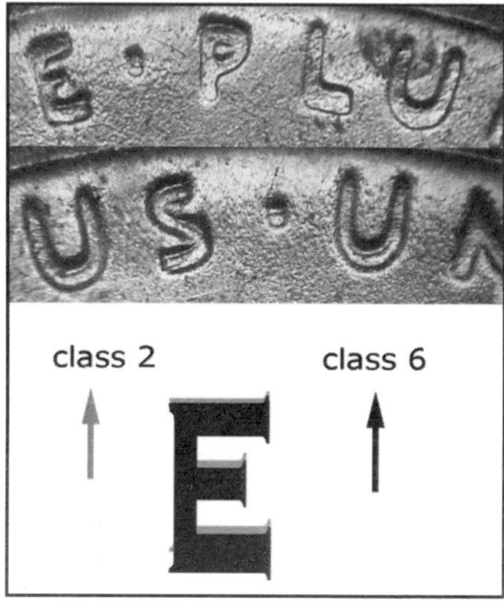

Non-collectible Doubling

A frequent problem beginning collectors confront is doubling on coins that is not hub doubling at all. Almost all of the doubling created on coins that does not come from the design on the die is referred to as machine damage doubling.

Machine damage doubling, or MDD, manifests itself in three basic forms, none of which has any collectible value by itself. Slight MDD flaws are a fairly common result of high speed coining presses and the many intricacies machines introduce to the coining of metal. They are so common, in fact, that there are a number of different years of coins that often show MDD in some form rather than a solid, clean strike.

The first form of MDD is strike doubling. This is the most common form of MDD and is generally attributed to a loose set screw in the die, which allows the die to bounce on the coin during coining. This bounce slightly doubles the design on the coin.

Strike doubling has a flattened appearance when compared to true hub doubling. Note also that it affects the mintmark as well, which does not happen with hub doubling prior to 1990. Photo by author.

The main characteristic difference between strike doubling and a doubled die is that strike doubling has a lowered, shelf-like appearance. On the other hand, a doubled die will show the roundness that the devices should have if they hubbed into the die out of alignment. In other words, doubling caused by the hub will have the same shape in relief as the normal design, while machine doubling will always have a flattened appearance.

The second characteristic that is always present on strike doubled coins is that the doubling will "take up" part of the overall profile, or width, of the devices affected. The outline of where the device meets the flat field of the design will be normal in all cases, and the doubling will be within the boundary of the thickness of a normal device.

Eject doubling is another form of doubling that happens on individual coins in the striking chamber and is not a part of the design on the die. It looks a lot like strike doubling, but it has one very telling characteristic not present on strike doubling; it shows a raised ridge next to the doubling.

Imagine the recesses of the die acting as scoops. When the coin is ejected from the chamber after being struck, the die is still stuck to the coin. The force of the ejection pushes the coin off the die creating the doubling.

The reverse of a 1968-D cent that shows strong eject doubling. Notice how the doubling appears to have been scooped up from the sides of the letters. Photo by author.

The last form of non-collectible doubling has a number of names and has fooled many collectors. It is called die deterioration doubling, or abraded die doubling. Although the two have slightly different causes, they look about the same in appearance, thus the terms are often interchanged.

This form of doubling is on the die, which means it is replicated from coin to coin, but is caused by wear or over polishing a die and not by the hubbing process. It is very common on some dates of Lincoln cents, especially 1946, 1949, 1953, 1954, and 1955. The latter of these is often sold for a few dollars per coin and is called the "Poor Man's Double Die." This is a misnomer, as these coins have nothing to do with hub doubling and are extremely common.

The main characteristic of this form of doubling is a "shadow" of raised field on the outside edge of the devices near the rim. On the many cases where this affects the date, usually only the last digit of the date is affected. On more heavily die worn examples, the entire date can be affected.

Heavy die deterioration doubling shows on this 1955 cent. These are extremely common cases of coins struck with heavily worn dies. Photo by author.

3 | GRADING LINCOLN CENTS

Grading is the term given to the activity of assessing a coin's condition based on circulation wear, environmental exposure, or damage that it has endured since it was minted. Imperfections in the dies and the striking process used to produce the coin become a factor as well when grading examples of uncirculated condition, or "mint state" coins. The current (and most accepted) scale of grading is based upon a 70 point system originally devised by Dr. William H. Sheldon during his authoring of the book *Early American Cents* (later renamed *Penny Whimsy*).

This system was given a scale of 1 through 70 with the higher numbers representing a higher grade and is subdivided into nine different categories for circulated or "worn" coins where gaps between the numbers will be noticed. When grading uncirculated coins (coins without wear) all ten digits between 60 and 70 are used so more accuracy can be achieved in describing the number of flaws on the coin. The absence of wear would otherwise warrant only one grade for both a nearly perfect uncirculated coin and an uncirculated coin with a scratched surface.

Uncirculated coins are by far the most difficult to grade, because for grades below uncirculated one must assess only the wear on the coin and the general appearance of the coin to give it a reasonably accurate grade. Uncirculated coins take practice to learn to grade because five different points of the coin's quality must be considered. They are: strike, surface, luster, marks, and eye appeal, the latter being the most subjective in nature.

Eye appeal is the most predominant factor in 'market grading,' the term used to define the assessment of the grade of a coin with market standards of rarity and value for that date and mintmark within that series. If the pool of comparative coins is generally low in quality, a market graded coin might receive a higher grade than its technical merits would warrant because its eye appeal is nicer to the grader than other similar coins of equal technical merit within that issue. Although eye appeal is still an important factor in technical grading, it is given much more weight in market grading.

Market grading is usually used on Lincoln cents for the issues that are typically lacking luster and detail. A good example is in early branch mint cents, especially those in the mid-1920s that rarely show full detail, and thus could not grade above MS-64 on a technical standard regardless of how mark-free and lustrous the coin may be.

Since it is niether fair nor realistic to assume that a certain date and mintmark cannot grade at higher grades simply because it does not compare in strike and detail to a similar coin minted decades later, market standards for that date and mintmark apply. For those issues, market grading applies not only to uncirculated specimens but to circulated coins as well, since the lack of detail exhibited by such coins struck at the same time already had technical points against it.

Because the majority of Lincoln cents are usually graded closer to the technical standard, this book focuses more on technical grading. Most of the series can be graded mainly on the technical merits of the coin because the majority of Lincoln cents are generally equal, considering the five points of grading previously mentioned.

Remember, when grading coins, no more than a five power loupe is necessary for assessing the grade of a coin. Any magnification higher than five power will reveal minor imperfections that would otherwise not be seen. Focusing on too small an area on the coin will affect your overall view of the coin and will skew your assessment of the coin's grade.

Lastly, a grade is a subjective opinion of a person's thoughts about the condition of a coin. It is not as much a science as it is an art. The more a person grades coins the more he or she understands the idea that grading is not necessarily black and white, right or wrong. The standard set forth by the ANA is an attempt to give a range of expectations one should have about a coin based on its grade. It is not a set of rules; it is a guide.

The Five Points of Grading

In grading uncirculated coins, the method I employ and the method that is taught here is to start at 70 (a perfect grade) with each coin and add or subtract points for qualities in five areas, with 70 being the highest possible grade and 60 being the lowest (except for cleaned or damaged coins). These five points are strike, marks, surface, luster, and eye appeal, in that order. This is not their order of importance, rather the order in which they are assessed.

For each of the five areas, the points taken or added are described in the text. Start at the beginning of this section and read through the end, assessing the obverse of a practice coin. When you finish with eye appeal, you should have a reasonably accurate grade assigned to the coin's obverse. Repeat this process for the reverse and then average the grade of the coin by weighing the obverse at 60 percent and the reverse at 40 percent.

If you are looking to grade circulated coins, see the section entitled, "Grading Wear."

Strike

Strike is the first determinant in grading coins. It concerns how heavy of an impression the coining press left on the coin when struck. Coins without full, complete detail — except those typically market graded — start at a grade of MS-64 (or PR-64) and work downward for other imperfections or upward for exceptional qualities in other areas. Those with complete detail can theoretically grade as high as MS-70, but rarely do.

In counting points downward from 70:

- Add one point if the strike is needle sharp and every detail shows perfectly.

- Take a point off if the strike is not superbly complete.

- Take three points off if the strike is slightly unclear at the high points.

- If there are detracting flat spots in the design that are not wear start at MS-64 and go to the next section.

Marks

Counting the number of hits, dings, or scratches (marks) on a coin is an important part of assessing a coin's grade. Simply count those marks that exist on the coin, assess whether they are major or minor, then subtract points from the overall grade of the coin based on where those marks are. This involves the prime focal areas, or the areas the eye sees first on a coin. See the map on the next page for a visual demonstration of these areas.

- Add a point if there are no detectable marks.

- Subtract a point for each minor mark in prime focal areas.

- Subtract two points for each moderate mark in prime focal areas or subtract a point for these marks in secondary areas.

- Subtract three points for each major mark in prime focal areas or subtract two points for major marks in secondary focal areas.

Marks should be assessed with care; a cluster of small marks may count as one moderate or major mark depending on the specific situation. Experience is the key factor in determining how many points to take for different marks in different areas. An entire book could be written on this subject alone.

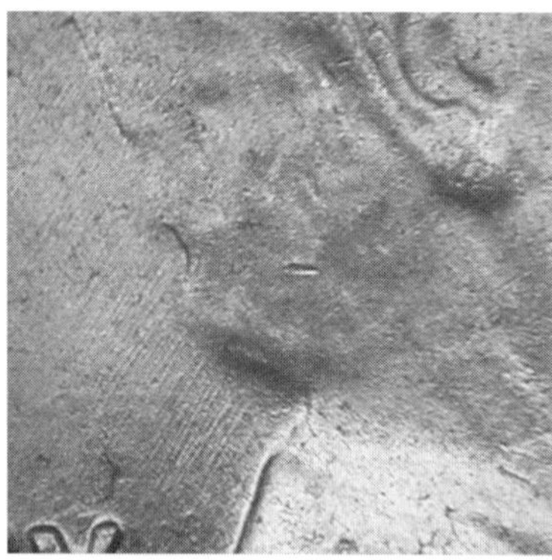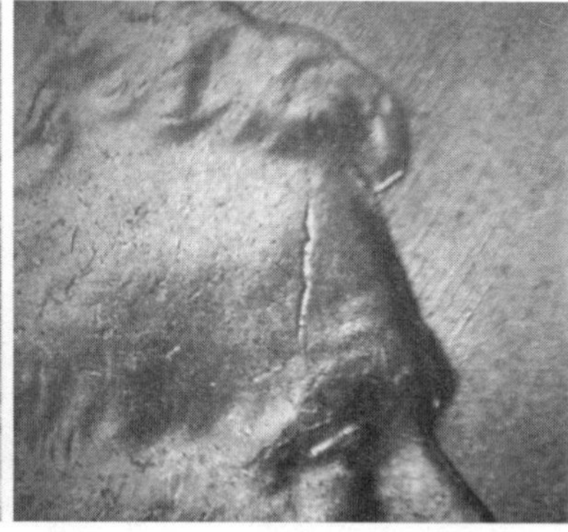

On the left is a small to moderate mark in the back of Lincoln's hair. It will be worth taking one point when grading the coin because it is in a secondary area. On the right a major mark in a prime focal area is worth subtracting three points. Photos by author.

Focal Areas of the Lincoln Cent

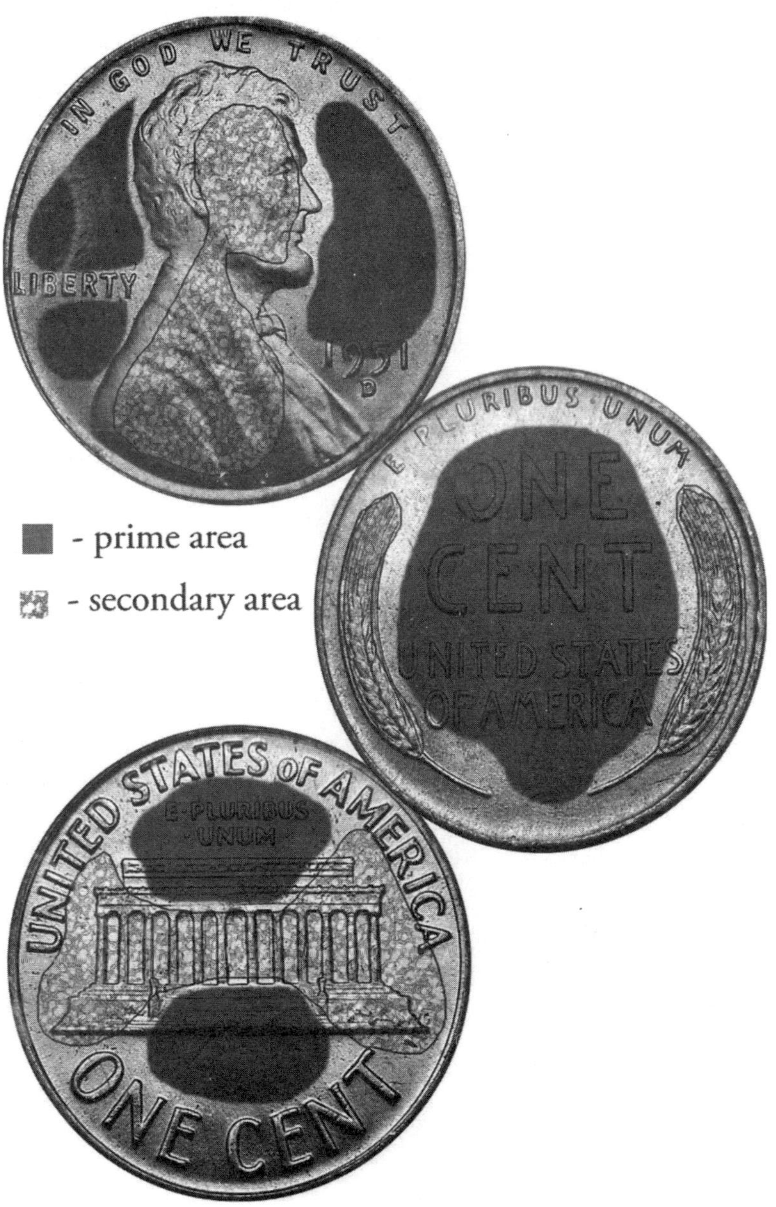

■ - prime area

▩ - secondary area

Surface

Grading the surface of a coin relates to looking at the overall texture of the coin. Is it mired with planchet imperfections? Is it cluttered with die scratches? Does it have a grainy appearance when you view it without magnification? Are there spots or blotches, such as carbon, that affect the coin?

- If the coin has a smooth, satiny surface with no negative impact add a point.

- If the coin has some texture problems, multiple die scratches, or minor planchet defects subtract one point.

- If the coin has moderate texture problems, large areas of die scratches, or more noticeable planchet defects, subtract two points.

- If the coin is noticeably marred by any of the above imperfections that detract from the coin to the naked eye, subtract three points.

Luster

In this area take into account how much the coin shines and how it shines. Is the coin dull, lifeless? Does it have a single axis of luster, or more than one axis of luster that is uneven?

- If the coin has brilliant luster with one axis point, add a point.

- If the coin has some brilliant luster but is impaired somewhat subtract a half point. This could include having an uneven axis of spin for the luster.

- If the coin has breaks in the luster or has large dull areas subtract one point.

- If the coin is dull and lifeless (and is not cleaned) subtract two points.

Again, this is another area that may take some experience to master. Luster is somewhat subjective and is usually not the same from one coin to the next. Take into account that this is not the area of most importance when grading, so take points sparingly.

Eye Appeal

This is by far the most difficult area to assess, because it requires knowledge of the series and the market for the series before one can truly tell whether the coin has positive, average, or negative eye appeal. It is the most subjective area of grading and lends itself more to the marketability (market grade) of the coin than to technical merits.

By the time you reach this point with a coin, you should have a number of points added or subtracted that note the qualities of the coin. If the eye appeal of the coin lends to that grade then little adjustment would be necessary. If the eye appeal is either far stronger or far weaker than the grade you reached suggests, it may be necessary to add or subtract points based on that alone.

Adding to eye appeal are such things as perfectly even color or attractive color, especially in the case of toning that forms perfect rings of color that fade into one another. This is called "bullseye" toning and is very desirable in the marketplace.

Another area for adding to eye appeal is earlier die state coins that have sharp details and a noticeable lack of die flow lines in the fields. Coins that are late die state may detract from overall eye appeal, because wear on the die contributes to softness in some details, and so points could be subtracted.

Other subtractions from eye appeal may come from blotchy spots, uneven color, or marks that detract from the overall look of the coin. If a major mark in a prime focal area only subtracts three points, this may not be enough to make up for a huge gash in an important area. It is acceptable to subtract another point for the same mark under the area of eye appeal.

In summary, it is completely up to the grader of the coin — whether he or she be professional, a dealer, or a collector — to determine how good a coin looks and to add or subtract eye appeal points based on what they think. It is impossible to explain every aspect of eye appeal because it is different for each individual grader and coin. Once again, experience is the key factor.

The Final Grade

Once the obverse and reverse are graded separately, multiply the obverse grade by six and the reverse grade by four. Add the two together and divide by ten. That's the final grade of the coin.

For example, take a coin with a 64 obverse and a 66 reverse:

64 x 6 = 384

66 x 4 = 264

384 + 264 = 648

648 / 10 = 64.8

With rounding, the coin grades MS-65.

The Color of the Coin

When grading uncirculated coins made from a predominantly copper based alloy, the color of the coin is described with the grade. Three different designations of color are used: red, red-brown, and brown.

For coins to be considered red, they must have at least a 95 percent tone of red on both sides of the coin. Coins are considered to be brown when 5 percent or less of the surfaces of the coin are red. The red-brown designation is used for all coins between these two criteria.

Toning in any color other than red is considered brown, thus a coin with natural color having less than 5 percent red color is considered to be brown.

An abbreviation is placed at the end of the coin's numeric grade to denote color — RD for red, RB for red-brown, and BN for brown. Typically, only uncirculated and proof coins will receive these notations. However, circulated coins in about uncirculated grade will sometimes receive these designations.

Case Study #1

OBVERSE

Strike: The mottled effect visible on the shoulder is from a mix of dirty dies and a rather soft strike. The lack of detail on the O of ONE on the reverse confirms that this is a soft strike. Since this is a San Francisco minted cent, the softness is expected. It's still going to take three points, because it is weak and cannot be ignored.

Marks: This coin is relatively free of marks. However, there is one distracting mark right on the center of the jaw line. It's worth a point. Another distracting area is a mark on the back of the neck. This is not in one of the focal areas, so it will be worth only one point.

Surface: An overall satiny coin with few problems other than the shoulder, for which we already removed a point in strike.

Luster: Although it cannot be shown in this book, the luster has a dual axis and is quite weak on the right side of the design. A point should be deducted for this.

Eye Appeal: Overall the coin has a few minor faults that detract from it. The even tones of the color (which naturally do not show here) add to the overall appearance of the coin. The good and bad points of eye appeal cancel each other out.

Overall Grade: 70 minus six points deducted = 64.

REVERSE

Strike: A good deal of weakness is observed in the typical spot: the O of ONE. Deduct two points for strike because the area that shows the softness is smaller on the reverse.

Marks: Not surprisingly, the reverse shows less bag damage than the obverse. One small area above the T of CENT deserves a point taken off.

Surface: Carbon spots in a few areas take an overall total of three points. They show up dark on the photo and are small but numerous.

Luster: Again, this doesn't show in the photo. The luster is slightly lacking due to the strike, but it is not bad enough for a point. It has one major axis and is rather even.

Eye Appeal: The spots and strike really detract from eye appeal. Because of this, a point comes off.

Overall Grade: 70 minus seven points deducted = 63.

(64 x 6) + (63 x 4) = 63.6

The coin has about 10% brown on the obverse, and 15% brown on the reverse. The overall final grade is MS-63RB.

Case Study #2

OBVERSE

Strike: 1909 Lincoln cents are usually struck very well, and this one is no exception. The only flaw in strike is that the LI of LIBERTY is not complete. No points taken or given.

Marks: This coin is relatively free of marks on the obverse, but it does have a couple of spots of carbon in front of the face, and a blotch near the rim above LIBERTY. Two total points for marks.

Surface: Typical surface for early Lincoln planchets. This one has some striping, which is a problem. One point taken.

Luster: The luster on this coin is lacking. There is little cartwheel luster even though the coin is not cleaned. Two points off.

Eye Appeal: Overall the obverse has little going in its favor for overall eye appeal. Nothing taken or given.

Overall Grade: 70 minus five points deducted = 65.

REVERSE

Strike: No weak points show, which is typical for the date. No points taken or given.

Marks: Rather large marks show on the E of CENT and one large hit shows on the first S of STATES. Take three total points for these.

Surface: The reverse surface looks nicer than the obverse. It is rather smooth and satiny, which is typical. No points taken or given.

Luster: Again, there is little luster on the reverse, just like the obverse. Take two more points.

Eye Appeal: No distractions, but no real allure as a beautiful coin. The slightly blotchy appearance of the coin is exaggerated by variations in shade in the photo and does not reflect the actual look of the coin. No points taken or given.

Overall Grade: 70 minus five points deducted = 65.

Since the obverse and reverse are the same grade, no need to do the math. The overall grade is MS-65.

The coin has about 15% red on the obverse, and 20% red on the reverse.

The overall final grade is MS-65RB.

GRADING WEAR

Assessing the grade of a coin with wear is far easier than grading uncirculated coins, because the amount of wear is the only factor to determining a coin's grade if there is no cleaning or other damage on the coin.

Studying the series and learning first hand what wear looks like are the only ways to learn how wear looks different from a soft strike, especially in grades from VF-20 through EF-40. These coins can take a great deal of patience to learn to grade effectively. Reading this book in its entirety will help you learn which dates are typically softly struck. This information will prove useful when you come across circulated issues where the softness of strike plays a role in any assessment regarding the amount of actual wear on the coin.

Coins that fit between categories of wear will normally be given a final decision based on eye appeal. At times, a grader will encounter a coin that bridges the tiny gap between a VF and an EF grade. If it is a nice looking, defect free coin with a bit too much wear for EF but not enough wear to appropriately call VF, then it could be assigned an EF grade. Conversely, those that have the same details yet do not have attractive eye appeal will normally be assigned the lower of the two grades.

A coin that has been cleaned or damaged is given a net grade, which is a lower grade assigned to a coin with otherwise better technical merits that exhibits problems that cannot be ignored. The net grade takes into account how much the overall coin is affected by the problem. Harsh cleaning or severe damage will result in a grade that is two letter grades below the technical merits of the coin. Lighter cleaning or light damage will result in a one-letter grade reduction of the overall grade. Examples of net grading are given at the end of the grading text.

About Uncirculated (AU)

A coin with a touch of friction or wear that has at least part of its original mint luster. Lower AU grades can show some flatness in the highest points of detail.

AU-58 - Most of the original mint luster will remain. A very light amount of friction is visible on the cheek, ear, and jaw. On wheat cents, a light amount of friction will be visible on the denomination and on the wheat stalks. On memorial cents, a very light amount of friction will show on the cornice and steps, as well as the planters on either side of the steps.

AU-55 - Most of the original mint luster will remain. Some light wear will show on the cheek, ear, and jaw, but these areas will not be flattened. On wheat cents, light wear will show on the upper wheat grains and wheat lines, but these areas will not be flattened. On memorial cents, a light amount of wear will show on the upper cornice, lower steps, and the planters, but these areas will not be flattened.

AU-53 - Half of the original mint luster will remain. Friction will be noticeable as spots without luster in the center of the fields that are not protected by devices. Lightly flattened spots will show on the cheek, jaw, and ear. On wheat cents, lightly flattened spots will show in the wheat grains. On memorial cents, lightly flattened spots will show on the planters, upper cornice, and the center of the lower steps.

AU-50 - About half of the original mint luster will remain. Friction will be noticeable as areas without luster in the center of the fields that are not protected by devices. Small flat areas will show on the cheek, jaw and top of the ear. Light flattening of the higher hair curls will be noticeable. On wheat cents, small flat areas will show on the wheat grains. On memorial cents, the planters will be worn nearly flat and the upper cornice will show small areas of flat wear. The center of the steps will show some flattening as well.

Close-up photos of wear on both sides of a typical AU coin. This one grades AU-55.

Extremely Fine (EF)

A coin with light wear that may have part of its original mint luster. Some flattening will be present on the higher points of relief.

EF-45 - Less than half of the original mint luster will show. Wear will be noticeable in the fields, as most areas not protected by devices will be lacking luster. The cheek and jaw will be worn flat in the center, and the top of the ear will be slightly flattened. Flattening in the hair curls will be noticeable. On wheat cents, the grains will have flat spots, but the wheat lines will be clear and bold, except on typically weak dates. On memorial cents, the planters will be worn flat, and flat areas will show along the cornice and cornice top. The center of the lower steps will be worn nearly flat.

EF-40 - Some original mint luster will show around protected areas, and the luster will be worn off in all other areas. The cheek and jaw will be noticeably flattened but completely separated, and the ear will be flat at the top, but the lower two-thirds will be completely separated from the hair. The hair curls in the center of the bust will be worn nearly flat but will still show detail. The coat line will be weak at the top and the lapel will show considerable flatness. On wheat cents, the grains will have flat spots but will be separated. The wheat lines will be clear but some spots will show weakness. On memorial cents, the planters will be worn nearly flat, and the lower center of the stairs will be flattened. The cornice will show some flat areas and the cornice top will be flat. The lower base, bushes, and columns will show light signs of wear.

Close-up photos of wear on both sides of a typical EF coin. This one grades EF-40.

Very Fine (VF)

A coin with light to moderate wear. Mint luster is gone. Flattened high points and worn fields in unprotected areas will be present.

VF-35 - Some original mint luster may be present but is not required. Flattening of the cheek and jaw areas is apparent, yet these areas will be completely separated. The ear will show some separation from the hair but will be flattened. Most of the hair curls will show some wear with the higher areas completely flattened. The coat nearly merges with the neck, and the lapel will be mostly flattened. On wheat cents, the wheat grains are worn nearly flat on top but will be separated. Some of the wheat lines may be weak but all will be separated. On memorial cents, the planters, center of the steps, and the center area of the cornice will be worn nearly flat but will show detail. The columns and bushes will show light areas of wear.

VF-30 - All of the mint luster will be gone except for very small parts of the field in very well protected areas. The cheek and jaw areas are flat with a depression between them. The ear will blend with the hair and most hair curls will be worn flat. The coat will merge with the neck in the center of the bust, and the lapel will be worn flat. On the wheat cent, the wheat lines will be considerably flattened and will show weakness to the point of being faintly visible. The wheat grains will be flattened and some will begin to merge. On memorial cents, the cornice top, planters, and steps will be worn flat and the columns and bushes will show some flattening.

VF-25 - All of the mint luster will be gone. The cheek and jaw areas are flat with a light depression between them. The ear will blend with the hair and most hair curls will be worn flat. The coat will merge with the neck in the center third of the bust, and the lapel will be worn flat. On the wheat cent, the wheat lines will be considerably flattened and will show weakness to the point of merging in small areas. The wheat grains will be flattened and some will merge. On memorial cents, the cornice top, planters, and steps will be worn flat, and the columns and bushes will show flattening.

VF-20 - All of the mint luster will be gone. The cheek and jaw areas are flat with a very light depression between them. The ear will blend with the hair and the hair curls will be worn flat. The coat will merge with the neck in the center two thirds of the bust, and the lapel will be worn flat. On the wheat cent, the wheat lines will be considerably flattened and will show weakness to the point of merging in areas. The wheat grains will be flattened and some will merge. On memorial cents, the cornice, planters, and steps will be worn flat and the columns and bushes will show flattening and slight loss of detail.

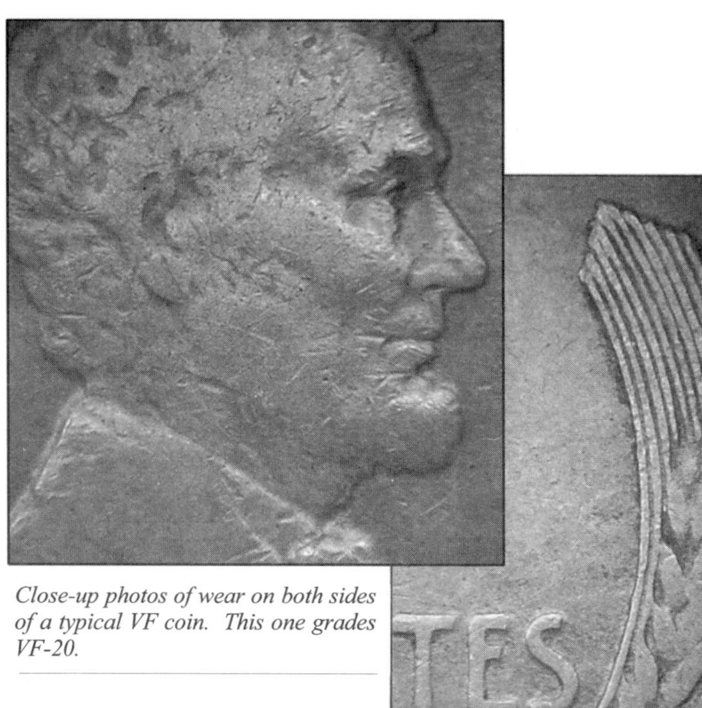

Close-up photos of wear on both sides of a typical VF coin. This one grades VF-20.

Fine (F)

A coin with moderate wear. All major design elements intact, however areas of higher relief are flat and lacking detail.

F-15 - The cheek and jaw areas are flat and will merge slightly. The ear will be flattened and will merge with the hair. The center of the head will be flattened with loss of detail in some areas. The collar will merge with the coat and neck, and the lapel will be worn flat and will merge slightly with the coat folds. On the wheat cent, the wheat lines will be mostly visible but will merge in areas. The wheat grains will be flattened and merging with one another. Memorial cents have rarely reached this grade.

F-12 - The cheek and jaw areas are flat and will merge. The ear will be completely flattened but will show some detail. The center of the head will be flattened with loss of detail in areas. The coat will show all major details but will be worn nearly flat. On the wheat cent, the wheat lines will be at least two thirds visible but will merge in areas. At least two-thirds of the wheat grains will be outlined. Memorial cents have rarely reached this grade.

Very Good (VG)

A coin with moderate to heavy wear. Most major design features show but are weak. Most higher relief areas are missing detail.

VG-10 - The cheek and jaw areas are flat and completely merged together. The outline of the jaw and bottom third of the ear will be visible. The center of the head will be flattened with loss of detail in many areas. The coat will show all major details but will be worn flat. On the reverse, the wheat lines will be at least one-third visible. At least one-third of the wheat grains will be outlined but they will be nearly flat and lacking detail.

VG-8 - The head will be flattened with loss of detail in many areas. The outline of the jaw and bottom fourth of the ear will be visible. The coat will show most major details but will be worn flat. On the reverse, some of the wheat lines will be visible. At least one-fourth of the wheat grains will be outlined but they will be flat and lacking detail.

Good (G)

A coin with heavy wear. Major design areas are missing most of their detail. All lettering is legible and not merging with the rim.

G-6 - The head will be flattened with loss of detail in all areas. The outline of the center of the jaw will merge with the neck. The very bottom of the ear will be visible but the remainder of the ear, except for the center, will be flat. The coat will show some major details but will be worn completely flat in the center. On the reverse, a few of the wheat lines will be visible. A few of the wheat grains will be outlined but they will be flat and lacking detail. The rim will be complete.

G-4 - The head will be flattened with loss of detail in all areas. The outline of the jaw will merge with the neck and will be barely visible. The coat will be worn nearly flat. The date will be completely legible and sharp. The devices around the edge of the design will be flattened but will not merge with the rim. On the reverse, a few of the wheat lines may be visible but the wheat stalks will be worn nearly smooth, only showing deeper areas of detail. The rim will be complete but weak in areas.

About Good (AG)

A coin with very heavy wear. All design elements worn to show only basic outlines. All lettering is legible but weak and is merging with the rim.

AG-3 - Only major design features remain. The date will be completely legible but weak. The devices around the edge of the design will be flattened and may merge with the rim. On the reverse, only major design features will show. The wheat stalks will be completely flat and will merge with the rim.

FR-2 - Many major design features will be flat and barely visible. Some of the lettering around the rim will be visible. The date will be partially visible and distinguishable. The reverse will be flat. The inner edges of the wheat stalks will be visible, as will most of the center lettering. The motto will merge with the rim and may be indistinct.

PO-1 - Barely recognizable as a Lincoln cent. The major features of the design will be visible but indistinct and partially gone. The date may not be legible. On the reverse, almost the entire design will be gone. Some of the lettering in the center of the design will be visible.

4 | DIE VARIETY ATTRIBUTION SYSTEM

Collecting die varieties involves using a system of die numbers to catalog each individual die that struck coins exhibiting the characteristics of a die variety. Coins can be compared to one another by the attributes and markers for a given die and assigned that die's number when a match is found.

Tedious effort was put into a die variety system that would work for all U.S. coins and that could be used within each denomination without interfering with the others. In 2001, Robert W. Frye and I developed what is officially referred to as the "USCV system" (United States Coin Variety) but is more commonly referred to as the "coppercoins system" because at the time www.coppercoins.com was the only entity employing the system.

Since die varieties encompass all examples of a short number of different types of anomalies, it was decided that a two-letter abbreviation would suffice in naming the type of variety exhibited by a die. This abbreviation, in combination with the date, mintmark, denomination, and the number given to the die in the order it was listed would provide a unique identification system for each die.

The first part of a die number lists the date and mint that produced the coin. The initial P is used for the Philadelphia mintmark regardless of whether the coin bears a mintmark. For all other coins the mintmark follows the date.

The second part of a die number lists the denomination in whole cents, then the type of anomaly being listed. Half cents receive a denomination of zero since they are the only denomination of coin issued in the U.S. lower than one cent. A nickel, for instance, is listed with the numeral 5 because it is five cents.

The anomaly type is one of six different die variety types. DO is given to doubled die obverses, DR to doubled die reverses, RD to repunched dates, OD to over dates, MM to repunched mintmarks, and OM to over mintmarks.

The third and last part of the die number is a three digit numeric identifier given to a die for that date and mint within that denomiation and die variety type in the order it was listed. Since the more obvious dies would be discovered and listed first, they generally have lower die numbers, but this is not always the case. Dies are always given a new number that follows the previous die listed.

If the die is a proof die, a P suffix is attached to the end of the die number. Proof dies are listed with all other dies by date and mint only, and are not listed separately because they are proof issues. It would be entirely possible (hypothetically) for 1964 quarter doubled die reverses to have a proof die listed as die number 002, and business strike dies listed for die numbers 001 and 003.

Examples of the system follow:

1904S-10DO-002: the second doubled die obverse listed for 1904-S dimes.

1884P-1RD-004: the fourth repunched date listed for 1884 Philadelphia Mint cents.

1964P-50DR-005P: the fifth listed doubled die reverse for 1964 Philadelphia Mint Kennedy half dollars, which happens to be a proof die.

1891S-100OM-001: the first listed over mintmark for 1891-S Morgan dollars.

These examples are offered as hypothetical examples of the scalability of the die system as a whole. However, at the time of this printing ONLY cents have been listed using this system. Check on the Internet at http://www.uscoinvarieties.com for updates on the use of this system.

5 | EFFICIENT SORTING

In order to use this book efficiently with a bag or mixed rolls of coins, it is recommended that you first sort them by date and mintmark. This will help avoid flipping from page to page looking for information and will also help you concentrate on one year at a time. This process will help you see some of the more minute differences in the coins of one given year by temporarily burning an image of the design for that year into memory.

The most efficient method I have found of sorting coins by year and mintmark involves a slight paradigm shift from the conventional method of sorting by decade first, then by year, then by mint.

Sorting Lincoln cents using the conventional method involves first sorting by decade. There are eleven decades for the Lincoln cent if you count the third digit in the date only and sort 1909 as its own decade. Sorting this way would involve eleven piles or containers in the first step.

In the second step, you would need another ten containers to sort the coins by specific date, and then you would have a third step to sort by mintmark. Altogether, this would involve well over 20 separate containers or piles to keep track of and store if you don't finish the entire job in one sitting.

With the more efficient model for sorting, label ten containers zero through nine and place them in rows of five (as shown in fig. 1, next page.) Sort the pile first by the last digit in the date only according to the numbers on the containers. All coins from 1910, 1920, 1930, etc. would go in the first container. All coins from 1911, 1921, 1931, etc. would go in the second container.

When this step is finished, you can store the last nine containers and work only with the first container and ten additional containers numbered in the same fashion. Sort again, only this time using the third digit in the date.

After completing step 2, you will end up with containers that are separated by date, and will only use 20 containers at a time to do so. Again store the last nine containers and you have one container with one date of coins inside to deal with. The only thing that remains to do is to sort each container by mintmark and you are ready to search through them!

This method may not be the best solution for sorting single rolls of coins, but for larger batches it saves a lot of time and is better organized for searching by individual date.

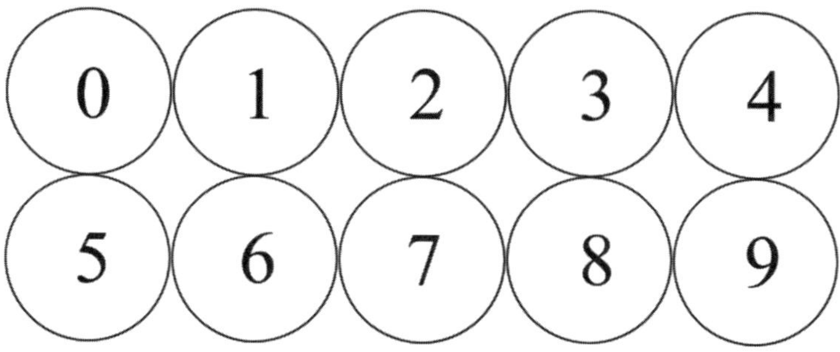

Fig. 1 - *sorting containers placed in order for either step in efficient coin sorting. In step 1, each container will hold all coins with years ending in the marked digit. In step 2, each container will hold all coins whose third digit matches the marked digit. At this point, the coins are sorted by year.*

6 | CHRONOLOGY OF THE LINCOLN CENT

THE EARLY YEARS: 1909-1933

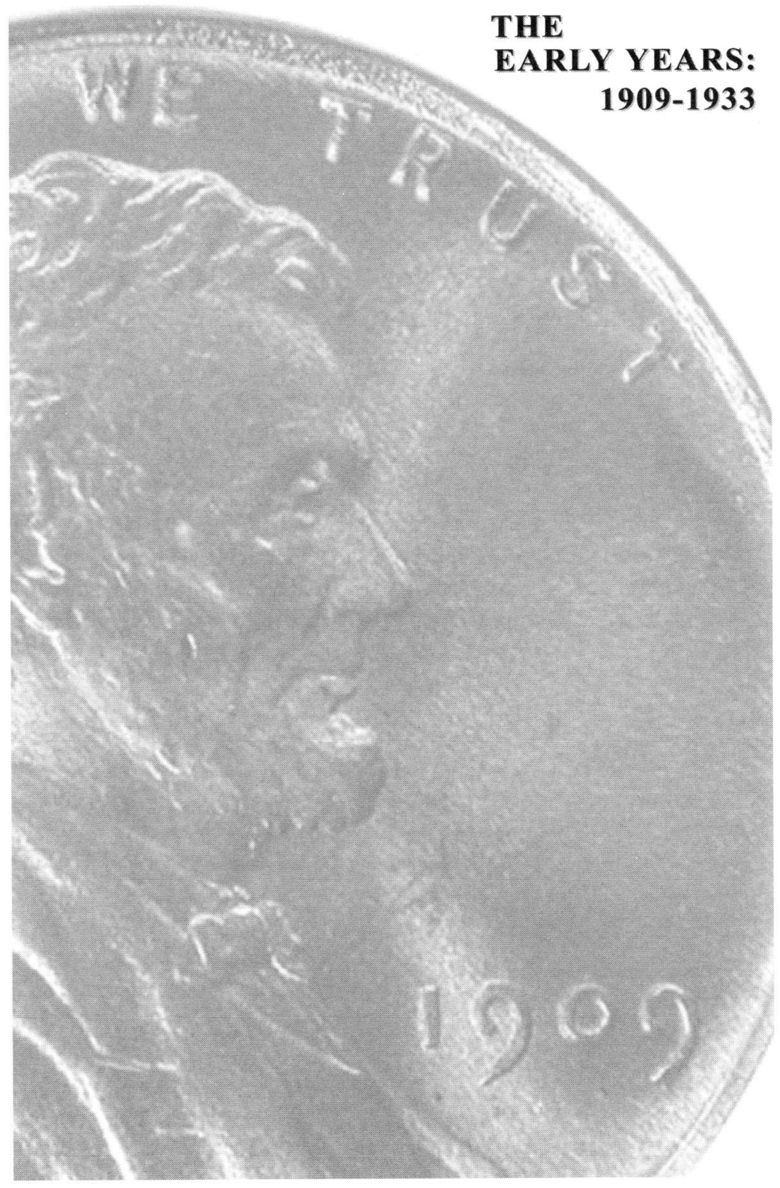

Overview

The period from 1909 to 1933 is referred to by many as "The Early Years." It was the launching pad for what was to become the longest running series of United States coinage ever. The Lincoln cent was the first U.S. coin issued for commerce with the likeness of a real person, President Abraham Lincoln. It was designed by noted sculptor and medal designer Victor David Brenner, and was commissioned by President Theodore Roosevelt in 1908.

Issued to commemorate the centennial of Lincoln's birth, the Lincoln cent was contested from its inception by legislators, press, and the public. Representative John Page of Virginia protested that busts of famous people were already everywhere, and when speaking of the likeness of Lincoln on the cent stated, "A further compliment they need not pay him."

A firestorm of debate over the designer's initials on the reverse of the new cent clouded the excitement over its release and caused mass hysteria among those trying to profit from the event. Press coverage was thick over the release of the new coin during the first week of August 1909, and rose to the level we would now expect of events such as the moon landing. Although changed slightly in its first week after initial release, the Lincoln cent survived this storm and went on to become the model for future coinage changes.

As with most other coin series of the time, many of the Lincoln cents from this period were circulated because of hard times. Both World War I and the Great Depression hindered coin collecting for aesthetic reasons and shoved coins into the hands of commerce where the vast majority were heavily circulated. The lack of higher grade coins from this time period has stunted the growth of knowledge in the area of micronumismatics, or the study of coins through magnification.

Although much is known about this era of the Lincoln cent, there is still much more to learn. Study your coins carefully — you may be the one to discover a new key.

1909

The first year of the Lincoln cent didn't come without problems. Public protest called for the immediate removal of the designer's initials (V.D.B., for Victor David Brenner) from the reverse of the coin shortly after its release to the public in August of 1909.

Although placing the designer's initials on coins was customary, the Mint obliged and removed the initials less than a week into production of the new cent. This caused the greatest mintage rarity among circulating cents to date with only 480,000 coins minted in San Francisco bearing the initials.

Other rarities exist in the more common non-V.D.B. variety of 1909-S cents. In addition to a couple of very well defined repunched mintmarks, another very curious RPM can be found. At first glance it may look like odd die damage, but on closer inspection it shows as a normal mintmark punched over a horizontal mintmark. Once you know what you are looking at, this die variety is quite prominent even in lower grades.

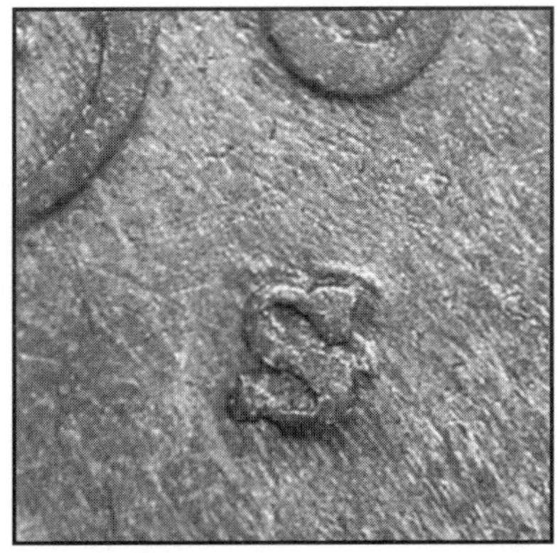

1909S-1MM-002 clearly shows the lower serif and lower curve of a secondary mintmark rotated 90° counterclockwise.

If you see odd, thin stripes of a different color of metal on a 1909 cent, it is not unusual. Many of the cents from this era show odd striping that often affects the entire planchet. These anomalies are often called "wood grain look," because the grain on the coin resembles that of wood. These were caused by impurities in the alloy mixture used to make the planchets and tend to affect a large number of cents minted prior to 1930.

Watch the S mint V.D.B. cents for counterfeits. Because of their rarity, value, and overall demand, they are the most counterfeited U.S. coin. It is highly likely that there are as many, if not more, counterfeits as there are genuine coins.

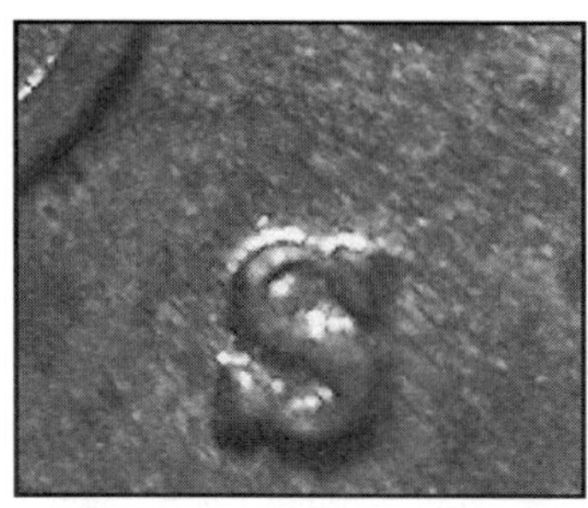

The correct shape for an S mintmark on all 1909 cents. Photo by Garry M. Naples.

The most common type of counterfeits are added mintmarks. The genuine mintmark for 1909-S and 1909-S V.D.B. cents have a unique shape when compared to that of later San Francisco minted cents. They all have a curl inside the upper serif, and the outer edges of the two serifs run straight vertically and are parallel to one another.

In addition, watch for fake V.D.B. initials added to the reverse of genuine S mint cents. They will usually have the wrong shape, especially in the B initial. Genuine 1909 V.D.B. cents will always have a downward pointing center stroke in the B initial. Counterfeits are known to typically have a straight horizontal center stroke.

Do not be confused if the exact shape of the initials or the placement of the dots between the initials appear different on 1909 cents minted with different dies. Comparison of the position and exact size and shape of the initials and dots from different dies indicates that they were not all hubbed into the dies from a common master, rather they were punched or engraved into each individual die. Compare the placement

Both photos are of genuine initials on 1909 cents. The top photo shows a Philadelphia minted cent and the bottom photo shows a San Francisco minted cent. Top photo by Richard S. Cooper, bottom photo by Garry M. Naples.

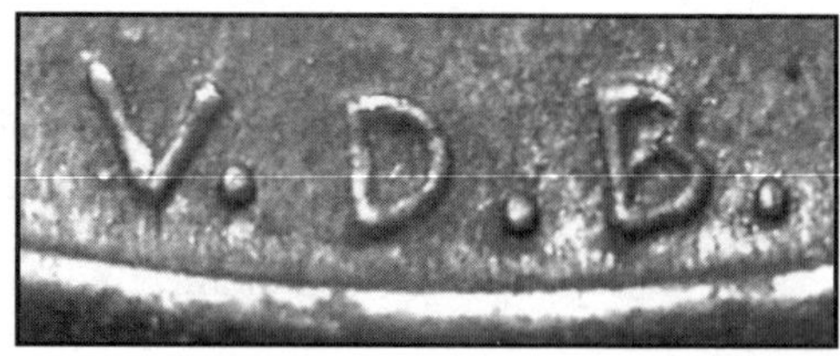

of the dot between the D and B of the initials in the photos for a visual understanding of this concept. The important thing to note is that the center of the B slants downward in both photos, as it does on all genuine coins.

1909 cents come with their share of doubled dies as well. Two distinct obverse doubled dies show on P mint V.D.B. variety cents.

1909P-1DO-001 is a class 4 offset hub doubled die with a nice spread to the northwest. Photo by author

Notice the thicker than normal devices on this doubled die. Since 1909P-1DO-002 is a class 6 (distended hub) doubled die, it does not show notching or separation lines common to other classifications of doubled dies. Photo by author.

1909P-1DR-001 is one example of a number of different doubled die reverse cents known for the plain version (no V.D.B.) of the 1909 Philadelphia mint cent. Note the clear separation in a number of the letters of the motto, as well as extra thickness in the left and right wheat lines. This mixing of doubling types gives this die an "added classification" status of distorted and distended hub doubling, class 2 + 6. Photos by author.

A faked 1909-S V.D.B. - added mintmark. ***Top***— *obverse and reverse photos of the entire coin. At first glance this looks like a valuable and popular 1909-S V.D.B. Lincoln cent.* ***Below*** *— The coin is a genuine 1909 V.D.B. cent with a glued-on mintmark. Notice how the mintmark is the wrong style for the date. These are likely just as common as genuine 1909-S V.D.B. cents, and many, like this one, are quite well executed. If the mintmark had been the right style for the date, this fake would be very deceptive, even to experts. Coin from Tom Fornicola, photos by author.*

1910

This year presents some very nice and very interesting RPMs, but not much of anything for doubled dies. Both RPMs are quite scarce and command a hefty premium in circulated grades, while the sheer value of a 1910-S cent in uncirculated outweighs much of the premium for an RPM in the same grade.

1910 cents are prone to the "wood grain look," which is just as strong in 1909 cents. The design is usually very strong and

1910S-1MM-002 shows a very nice north spread.

very clear. In many cases the fields will have a very slight mottled effect on both sides, and many people mistake them for the matte proof cents. The main difference that is easiest to detect on the matte proof cents is their square, sharp rim. The business strike cents do not have this sharpness.

The S mint cents have been faked, but not nearly as often as with the 1909-S cents. The most common form of fake is a 1940-S cent with a shaved 4, usually done crudely and on higher grade circulated to uncirculated coins. They are easy to spot; the 0 digit on genuine 1910 cents is much larger than on 1940 cents, and the digits of the date are evenly spaced. Faked 1940 cents have a very wide space between the nine and one digits where the diagonal of the four used to be. The entire bust is also higher in relief yet less detailed than on 1910 cents. In addition, the rims are much thinner on 1940 cents than on genuine 1910 cents. These fakes are quite scarce, yet do exist and will catch you by surprise if you are not cognizant of them. See the figures on the next page for comparison.

A less common yet much more dangerous counterfeit is the added mintmark. 1909-S cents are commonly faked in this manner, and the value difference between 1910 plain and 1910-S cents is quite large, especially in higher grades. The faked mintmarks are usually glued on, and a dab of acetone on a cotton swab rolled over the mintmark will usually lift them right off. Examination of the mintmark under a 30 power microscope will usually show the seam between the field and the added mintmark.

A curiosity for thrill seekers is the reported existence of coins that have a shadow of the V.D.B. initials on the lower reverse, where they should be expected on 1909 cents. A number of these have been reported to me for examination, but none of them showed anything more than die scratches or hits on the coin that wore to give the appearance of relief. Photographs of these reported "1910 V.D.B." cents have been published, but none of them show anything definite and convincing. Obviously the jury is still out on this phantom's existence.

Above is a 1940S cent crudely transformed into a 1910S cent. Notice the scrape marks left behind where the diagonal of the 4 should be, and notice the size of the zero digit. A genuine 1910 cent is below for comparison. Photos by author.

1911

As with the previous two years, 1911 cents are generally quite sharp. However, with branch mint coins especially, there is a noticeable tendency toward weaker details and weak mintmarks. Coupled with the same planchet quality problems that have plagued the series since its beginning three years earlier, the lower quality produced by the more worn dies makes for some interestingly ugly coins.

Even though this is the first year of cent production for the Denver Mint and the first cents ever to sport a D mintmark, their quality is less than that of the first cents minted in San Francisco a few years earlier. In a number of cases, coins that grade very fine or below require magnification and some imagination to figure out whether they were minted in Denver or San Francisco.

Mintmark varieties tend to take a turn for the worse this year as well. Very few are more than just noticeable through a 16 power loupe. Considering both mintmarked issues of 1911 are semi-keys to the series, it is surprising that none of the repunched mintmarks stand out as being especially rare for the date. The fact that many of the coins were minted with worn dies in lower quantity than other years, and that a large number of these coins were heavily circulated, lends to the fact that die varieties for this year are seldom of high quality or high grade.

There is, however, one very nice hunter's delight for this year. The earliest over mintmark (OMM) known in the Lincoln cent series is a lightly punched D/S with a moderate south spread. Listed as 1911D-1OM-001, this gem of a mintmark variety does not come without controversy. While some organizations, such as coppercoins.com, recognize it as an over mintmark, others list the die as a repunched mintmark. It is my opinion that the secondary mintmark is fully curved at the bottom with an upward pointing serif on the left side of the curve, fully indicative of the shape of an S, not that of a D. Moreover, computer image overlays show that the secondary mintmark on the example in coppercoins.com files matches nearly perfectly with the S mintmark punch used on 1911-S cents, and is completely void of the lower serif shape expected of a D punch. As with many other controversial die varieties, collectors will ultimately have to judge this one for themselves.

Overall planchet quality, die quality, and strike are all detrimentally poor this year, leading to an largely unexciting year of production. If it were not for the single OMM and branch mint coins that were minted in low quantity producing semi-key issues, 1911 would be an all but forgotten year for the Lincoln cent.

1911D-1OM-001 is noticeable as an OMM with the lower part of an S mintmark punch to the south. The shape of an S mint serif is clearly visible left of center just touching the bottom of the D mintmark. Photo by author.

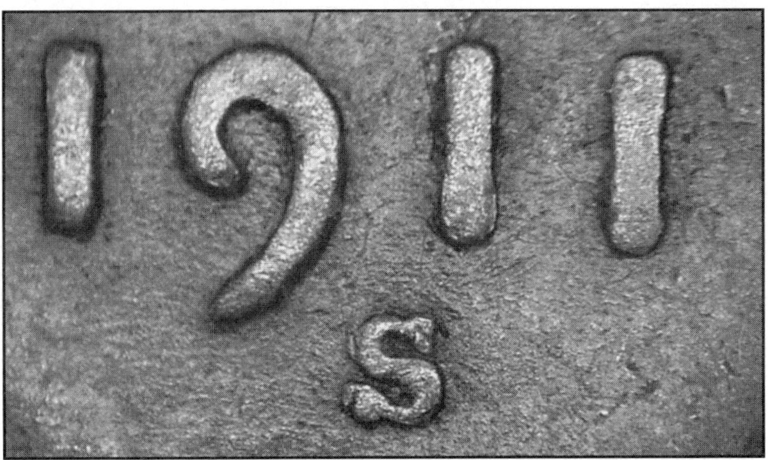

1911S-1MM-001 shows nice doubling toward the northwest. This repunched mintmark, as well as most other early date Lincoln cent repunched mintmarks, commands a high premium because of rarity. This particular die variety sells for over $50 in Fine condition. Photo by author.

1912

On the whole, quality of production this year is about the same as 1911's coins. Philadelphia minted coins tend to be of higher quality than the branch mint coins. The main difference this year is that planchet quality seems to be a little better than before.

Die varieties are scarce in number on 1912 cents and mintmark varieties are generally lackluster, although one S mint repunched mintmark does make enough of an impact to easily warrant premium value and collectibility. This S mint is also quite scarce, especially in grades above fine.

Watch 1912 plain cents for satin proofs — although very uncommon, they have been found offered as business strike coins. Just remember the sharp edged rim and clearer, sharper details for the proofs.

Overall, 1912 has a very limited selection of known die varieties worth hunting.

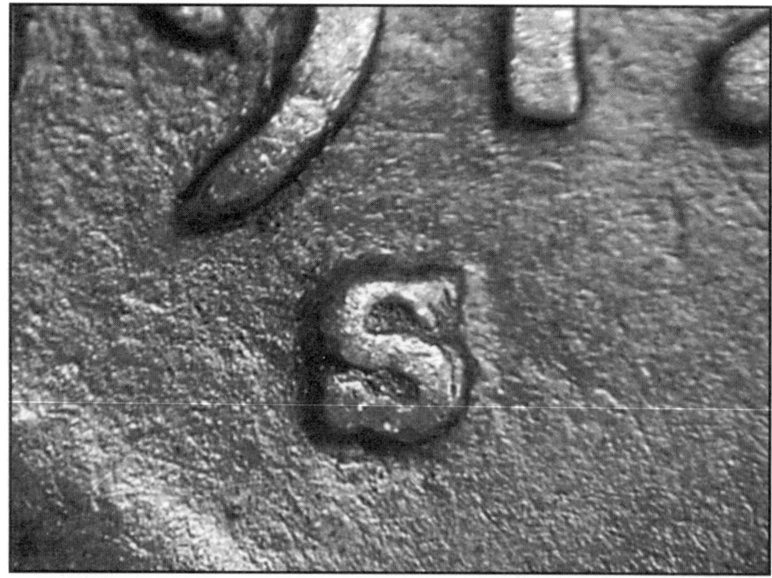

1912S-1MM-001, although not spectacular, is the best repunched mintmark for 1912. In this photo you can see the rather close northeast spread. Photo by author.

1913

It seems the downhill slide that started in 1912 picked up steam in 1913. Virtually nothing of note has ever been reported for 1913 cents. The only high point for the year is the lack of production at the branch mints, which kept mintage numbers rather low. This translates to rather high values for better grade coins today.

The overall quality of 1913 cents is mixed. Nicely struck examples with full, sharp detail exist, as do others struck by very worn dies. My suggestion is to always look for the sharpest detail possible on a cent, especially if you are looking for a higher grade example and are paying higher grade prices for it.

A 1913-S cent struck with extremely worn dies. This coin was reported as a possible repunched mintmark, but as the 9 in the date shows, this coin is exhibiting extreme die stress, not an RPM. Photo by Richard S. Cooper.

1914

The 1914 cent is usually found with better detail than 1911 through 1913 cents, and has always been more sought after than other dates in the teens. In fact, for many years after its release, the 1914-D and S mint cents were considered to be the key issues of the series, outweighing 1909-S and 1909-S V.D.B. cents in value by nearly double, even though their mintage was much higher.

As for items of note to look for, if it had not been for the 1914-D cent's very low mintage, this year's cents would be right on the bottom with 1913. There has been virtually nothing of note reported on 1914 cents regarding die varieties.

The major issue to watch for in this year's cents is counterfeit 1914-D cents. Because of their high value and demand, they are one of the most counterfeited U.S. coins. The most common method of counterfeiting these is by shaving the left half of the first 4 digit down on a 1944-D cent to make it look like a 1 on a 1914-D.

Above, a 1944-D cent shaved to look like a 1914-D cent. Compare the spacing in the date and the overall appearance of the details on the coin to the genuine 1914-D cent below. Genuine 1914-D photo from the Stewart Blay collection.

These are very easy to spot; the date has an awkward space where the 4 was shaved, the bust is too high in relief and lacks detail, and the rims are not thick as is common on 1914 cents. In addition, the most telling sign of all is that 1944 cents have the V.D.B. initials on the truncation of Lincoln's shoulder, a feature that was not on 1914 cents. The initials were added to the obverse in 1918. With little practice, the fakes are usually easy to spot. However, authentication is the key. If you are not certain, don't buy it.

The other common method of counterfeiting, like the 1909-S issues, is by adding a mintmark to a genuine 1914 cent. These are much more dangerous than the shaved 1944-D cents because all the details on the coin will match a genuine 1914-D cent, except for the mintmark itself. If you are going to buy an uncertified 1914-D cent, examine the mintmark area very carefully for seams, and make certain that you know the proper mintmark style used in 1914. It is narrow and usually sits in a depression caused by the mintmark punch. Added mintmarks will usually not have this depression.

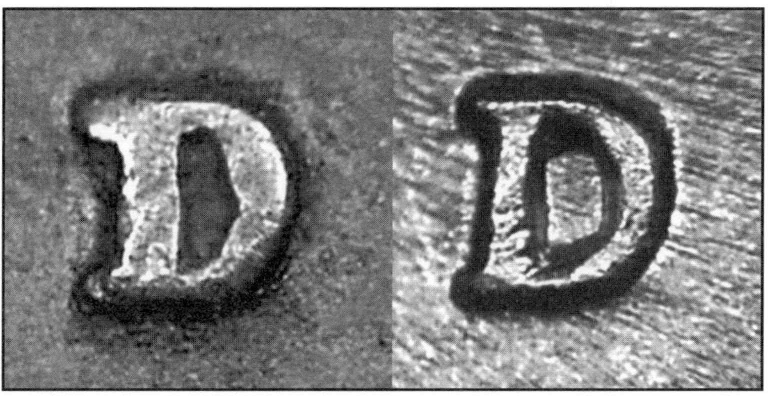

On the left is the proper mintmark style used on cents between 1911 and 1932. On the right is the mintmark style introduced in 1933.

1915

Save for a couple of minor repunched 1915-D mintmarks, 1915 proved to be another uneventful year for die varieties. This year's cents are usually of average quality and strike and are generally just plain boring.

A report came in last year that an experiment with a slightly different alloy was tested in 1915. The report states that the experiment did not work out well and was discontinued that year, but not before a number of these coins reportedly made it into circulation. This is supposed to answer for a number of striped color planchets, but I have never seen anything to confirm this report other than a "wood grain" look, which by all appearances is the same as the "wood grain" look of earlier cents.

Once again, since satin proofs were minted this year, watch for the possibility of being offered one as a normal business strike cent.

1916

Branch mint cents from this year tend to be of better quality than previous years and are rather difficult to find in higher grades. Philadelphia Mint cents tend to be very well struck and are fairly common in higher grades.

As for die varieties, this date has nothing to offer. Not a single doubled die or mintmark variety has ever been reported. Of all the years in the early Lincoln cents, the Mint did its best job of inspection and production this year.

Although quite rare, proof cents are still a possible find in bins and bags, although none have been reported as having been found this way. The same rules that applied to other early satin proofs would apply for this date — sharp rims, mottled fields, and very sharp details. 1916 was the last year proof cents were officially manufactured until 1936.

1917

The U.S. was deeply involved in World War I by 1917 and demand for new cents was greater than ever. This shows in a near-doubled production from 1916. It also tends to show in the quality of Denver and San Francisco cents, which are usually found with soft details from overworked dies.

The need for increased production could be the reason why a strong doubled die was skipped by mint inspectors and went into production. The earliest known major doubled die of the series affecting all areas of the design was minted in Philadelphia this year.

Although very scarce to rare, this doubled die is known in most grades from good to uncirculated. The uncirculated specimen almost had to have been saved by chance since doubled dies would not be studied or collected for another 40 years.

Because this doubled die is visible even in the lowest grades, it is still available in circulated mixtures and is found by collectors on a frequent enough basis to warrant mention here. Below are photos of the doubled die as it appears on higher grade coins.

This photo of 1917P-1DO-001 shows very nice doubling in the date. Since this is a class 5 pivoted hub doubled die with a pivot point near the lower left part of the design, the doubling shows well in the date and motto, but is not as strong in LIBERTY. Photo by Billy Crawford.

1918-1920

Combined because of very similar circumstances regarding quality, mintage, and die varieties, 1918 through 1920 proved to be quite dull years for the Lincoln cent. Very few die varieties have been reported for cents from these years, probably due to lack of quality found in most Denver and San Francisco minted cents.

Production numbers increased to record numbers by 1919 because of a war shortage of circulating coinage, and specimens are easy to find today in all circulated grades. Because of poor quality in all branch mint cents, however, finding nice, red examples with sharp details is all but impossible. High grade uncirculated examples of S mint cents from these years sell easily at levels higher than that of 1909-S V.D.B. cents of the same grade.

In contrast, Philadelphia minted cents from all three years tend to be plentiful even in uncirculated grades and can even be found in GEM state. In fact, just one example of a 1919 Philadelphia cent in MS-69 is known (see next page for photo).

Mintage dropped at all three mints in 1920, but not enough to greatly affect their availability. They are, however, less obtainable than 1918 or 1919.

These three years proved to be the last of high mintage for years to come. They would also be the last for another three years in which all three mints made cents. Rolls of all three years are still readily available in circulated grades.

1918 marks the first design change of the Lincoln cent. Although tiny, the cent designer's initials, V.D.B., were quietly placed on the truncation of Lincoln's shoulder on the obverse. The three small letters were so indistinct it would take years for collectors to discover them. After nine years without credit to the designer, the addition was more than deserved; all other circulating U.S. coins at the time displayed their designer's initials. The initials V.D.B, though tiny, remain on the coin today.

On a Page of its Own...

The single earliest known specimen of a PCGS certified MS-69 cent is this 1919 plain cent. Absolute and exquisite beauty exemplifying what a Lincoln cent should be shines brightly on this near-perfect specimen. If any coin deserves its own page in this book, it would be this one for obvious reasons. My thanks to the Stewart Blay collection for sharing this image with me. This one is a true pleasure to display for others to enjoy.

1921

In 1921 the Mint concentrated its efforts on accelerating production of silver dollars. Consequently, production of other coins, including the cent, fell dramatically compared to previous years. The Denver Mint made no cents this year, and the mintage at the Philadelphia and San Francisco Mints dropped to levels nearing one-tenth of 1920 production numbers.

Due to the lower production numbers, 1921-S cents are considered a semi-key in the series. Moreover, the poor quality of dies and planchets used to strike the 1921-S cents left few specimens in a condition exceeding MS-65, making this coin especially desirable in higher grades.

Workload shifted from the San Francisco Mint in 1921 to the Denver Mint in 1922. This caused some speculative hoarding of 1921-S cents; however, rolls have not been readily available for a number of years. Circulated rolls of 1921-S cents typically sell at $50-$75 when offered.

Aside from strike quality, there is nothing to mention regarding 1921 cents. No doubled dies or mintmark varieties have ever been reported for this date. This is likely due to their low mintage and low survival rate in higher grades.

Because of low mintage, lack of substantial hoarding in the early years, and overall low quality of what was produced, 1921-S cents are now highly sought after in higher grades. Examples like this one grading EF sell for over $15.00 in today's market. Photo by author.

1922

The only year in which all Lincoln cents were minted in one facility didn't come without problems. Due to faulty machinery and a lack of dies for the number of coins struck, almost all 1922-D cents show die wear to extreme levels and are horridly ugly. Some of these 1922-D cents, however, gained a lot of attention over the years that followed.

The lack of quality control over minting cents in Denver during 1922 caused some errors that for any other year would have gained little if any attention. If a mintmark were filled in on a die from a branch mint of any other year, the coin would have been tossed aside as the more common Philadelphia Mint issue — which of course has no mintmark. But in 1922 there were no cents minted in Philadelphia, which helps explain the mass hysteria over such an ugly issue as the 1922 "no D" cent.

Some of the coins were struck with dies so worn and filled with debris that the mintmark was nearly or completely invisible. Because a very limited number of dies (three in all) exhibited this problem, belief among the public was initially that there had been a very limited number of cents struck as Philadelphia issues. Interest soared for these coins, mainly because people didn't understand at the time that these were not Philadelphia issues, and that they were not purchasing a very low mintage coin. They were instead buying into what has become one of the largest fiascos in collecting Lincoln cents.

Although the current general acceptance in the market is that there was one of the three die pairs used that actually never had a mintmark in the beginning, this cannot be proven because there is no official record of the error, as there is no official record of any error.

It is my opinion that all 1922 "no D" Lincoln cents are common, grease filled or worn out dies, and that none of them should have ever gained the attention or value they currently demand.

Regardless of anyone's opinion, including mine, the fact remains that there is a strong market for what is known as "die #2," or the "strong reverse variety," of 1922 cents without a mintmark. The other two known die pairs have recently (within the past 30 years) been written off as extreme die wear on normal 1922-D cents and have lost most of their value, currently selling for under $25 in circulated grades.

The main difference between the three is that die pairs 1 and 3 have extremely worn reverse dies, to the point that the wheat lines are all but completely obscured even on uncirculated specimens, and die pair 2 has a rather normal detailed reverse and no sign of a mintmark.

There are many fakes, and there are still many examples of other 1922-D cents that have extremely worn obverse dies, with almost no mintmark remaining, that people unwittingly buy and sell as genuine 1922 "no D" cents. If you are going to pay the lofty prices asked for the controversial 1922 "no-D" error, then the key to surviving in the market is to ONLY buy certified, properly attributed coins.

A 1922 "no D" cent from the die pair recognized as die #2, or the "strong reverse." The reverse on this die pair is a typical full detail reverse, versus the washed out dull reverse with no wheat lines exhibited by both of the other recognized die pairings. This is the only one the market recognizes as being valuable. Photo courtesy of the Stewart Blay collection.

1923

There are some years in cents that are completely uneventful, and 1923 is one of them. There is nothing to mention regarding die varieties for this date; none has been reported. As for quality, this year is yet another in a chain of years that typically exhibit a number of problems related to die wear.

Mintage figures support that the Mint was still more concerned with silver dollar production than with Lincoln cent production. Even though far more cents were produced in 1923 than in 1921 and 1922, production was still far less than during the 1918-1920 period.

Denver did not mint any cents in 1923, so production of cents for the entire Western half of the country was left to the ill-equipped San Francisco Mint, which produced just less than 9 million pieces. Because of constraints in equipment and tools , overall quality of coins produced is quite poor. Very late die state coins are much more common than clean, crisp examples.

This is an example of the detail found on typical 1923-S cents. Notice how the obverse appears to grade a low very fine while the reverse details indicate an about good coin. This coin actually grades VF details net Fine because of the scratch on the reverse from STATES to AMERICA. The defect in and around the N of ONE is lamination, caused by impurities in the alloy used to make the planchet. This is rather common for early Lincolns. Photo by author.

1924

With few exceptions, this year's cents are remarkably similar to the previous few years. One of the exceptions is that the quality of detail on the cents this year appears somewhat better than that of the previous few years, although more stringent quality measures would be needed to bring them back up to the quality of the coins minted in the teens. Another exception is that for the first time in three years, all three mints were back in the business of producing cents. What's more, there are actually a few known die varieties to watch for in 1924 cents.

This year boasts the earliest known really nice distended hub doubled die in the series. On the reverse of a small number of coins there exists strong extra thickness on the entire motto and both wheat stalks. There has been only one of these coins reported to coppercoins.com, so the number actually made or still in existence is likely quite low. Other similar yet less noticeable doubled dies can be found on the obverse and reverse of both 1924 plain and S mint cents.

The five-year gap in repunched mintmarks comes to an end this year as well with a nice, wide south spread S mint RPM.

1924P-1DR-001, a class 6 distended doubled die reverse, shows moderate to strong extra thickness on all outer devices. Notice especially that the dots separating the parts of the motto are egg-shaped instead of their intended circular shape. This is the earliest such die reported to coppercoins.com. Photos by Bob Piazza.

1925

Although quality is still somewhat lacking in cents this year, it is noticeably improved over that of the early twenties. Far better detail can be expected out of Philadelphia minted cents, and at least somewhat better quality control shows on Denver Mint cents. San Francisco minted cents, however, still suffer from the same fatigue and mixed quality that has plagued them for the past three years.

Uncirculated specimens from Philadelphia are quite common, but the branch mint cents tend to be quite elusive in full-red mint state. San Francisco minted cents are quite rare, fetching prices in the thousands for GEM specimens.

What the Mint gained in their overall die quality they lost in die inspection. This year boasts a real nice lineup for die variety hunters. Nearly half a dozen strong repunched mintmarks start the lineup, and the heavy hitter is a super strong and quite scarce doubled die obverse.

On the facing page are photographs of two of the stronger repunched mintmarks for the date. While the Denver Mint seemingly did not create any repunched mintmarks this year, the San Francisco Mint has a number of impressive examples. This could be because mintmarks were punched into the dies in groups before shipment to the branch mints, meaning there is at least some likelihood that all the S mint RPMs for the date could have been created in one sitting.

Be careful when attributing RPMs on 1925-S cents. Two of them are very close in appearance and spread, although the giveaway that they are from different dies is in the relationship of the position of the mintmark compared to the date. This is an important factor in attributing all mintmark varieties. While the general appearance of the RPM could change with die wear, the position of the mintmark never changes. Remembering this can assist you as the first method of comparison when trying to prove or disprove that two coins were minted with the same die.

Only one doubled die is known for 1925, on an S mint cent obverse. It is a strong class 6 distended hub doubled die thus does not show separation lines.

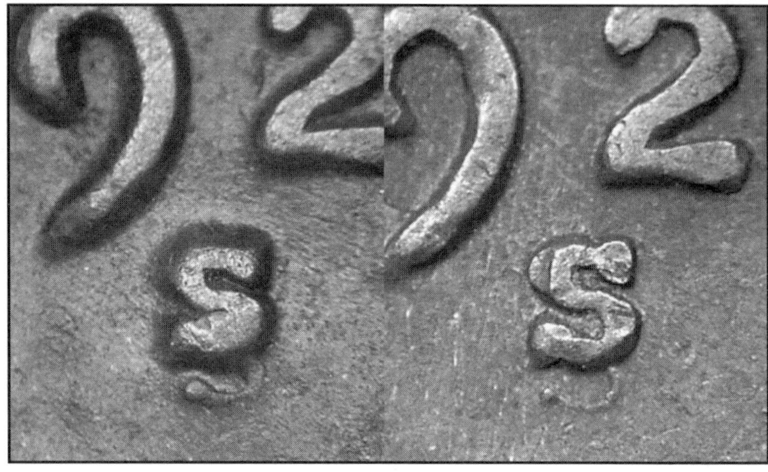

Two of the nice repunched mintmarks for 1925-S. On the left is 1925S-1MM-001, and on the right is 1925S-1MM-003. Although the attributes of these die varieties appear similar, they are different. Notice the deeper secondary punch on the left while on the right the spread is greater. Also notice that the position of the mintmark is slightly different between the two in relation to the date. Photos by author.

1925S-1DO-001 shows extreme extra thickness in the date, motto, and LIBERTY. This photo shows the date. Photo by author.

1926

In 1926, San Francisco mintage dropped significantly from 1925 levels and there was no improvement in the overall quality of the coins produced. While circulated examples are rather easily obtainable, mint state specimens, especially those in GEM grades with full detail, are very rare. For this reason, 1926-S is considered one of the semi-keys of the Lincoln cent series.

The Denver and Philadelphia Mint coins are quite a bit more obtainable. Although the overall quality of Denver minted cents is low, nice specimens with full detail are available. The Philadelphia Mint cents usually exhibit full detail and are available in most grades. Original mint state rolls are known to exist today.

Although 1926 is an illustrious year for the difficult to obtain higher grade branch mint coins, die variety hunters will find this year completely unimpressive. Not one single die variety has been reported for this date. Much of this probably has to do with their relatively low survival rate caused by widespread economic depression and a lack of collector interest at the time in saving what was recognized as low quality coinage.

1927

Quality of production saw an increase this year and, except for San Francisco issues, the number of cents minted decreased. Philadelphia Mint issues are common and can be found in high quality. Denver Mint coins are reasonably obtainable in much better quality than in previous years. San Francisco examples still suffer from die quality problems, and because of rather low mintage, are very difficult to find in higher grades. Circulated specimens of all three mints are easily obtainable.

Die variety hunters are in for a couple of treats this year. A rather nice doubled die obverse is scarce but obtainable on Philadelphia searches, while the earliest "doubled eyelid" doubled die coupled with a strong RPM can be found in Denver Mint coins.

In fact, the RPM exhibited on this die is the earliest known example of a classic "tilted" spread. This means that the first mintmark punched in the die was not flush with the surface of the die and was weak in points. The weak mintmark edge was repunched with the punch purposefully cocked in the opposite direction to strengthen the overall appearance of the mintmark, but was not directly in line with the first punching, thus creating doubling. Because it is not possible to tell which punching was first, and because the nature of the repunching prevents us from giving the repunching a cardinal direction, it is called "tilted."

1927D-1DO-001, doubled eyelid: Look for the bulge near the lower eyelid that is parallel to the upper eyelid. This is a wide spread weak hubbing of the upper eyelid. On the same die is 1927D-1MM-001, a very strong D/D tilted repunched mintmark. Notice that no matter how you look at it, neither mintmark is north or south of the other. This is a classic tilted spread. Photos by author.

1928

Little changed from 1927 to 1928 in quality or quantity of coins minted. Philadelphia minted cents are still of better quality than the branch mint cents, and San Francisco cents tend to have more problems than either of the other two.

A couple of interesting features show on 1928 cents, but for the better part, this year is rather void of significant die varieties. A rather nice tripled eyelid shows on some 1928-P cents, and nearly half a dozen different repunched mintmarks can be found, mainly on S mint cents. The number of die varieties is still limited because not only are there a limited number of dies used to mint the coins, but the mass production of the Lincoln cent still had not begun.

An interesting feature for this date is the fact that there are two different sizes of mintmark available on the S mint cent. Although a minor difference, it was discovered and studied in the 1930s, not long after its release. Different studies report various ratios of scarcity between the two, but it is without question that the large S is quite a bit scarcer than the small S.

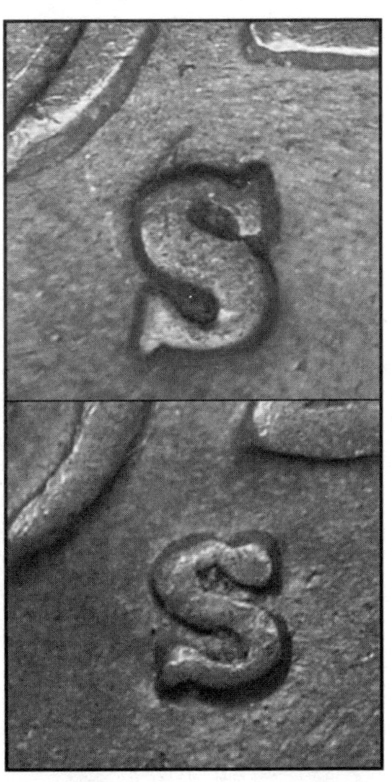

Top: *large mintmark.* **Bottom***: small mintmark.*

Collector interest is still quite modest for the different mintmark sizes. Both can be purchased from most dealers at the same price, but because of increasing interest in the series as a whole and an increase in collector population, the large S cents will eventually gain their own market and be listed separately at higher values.

An interesting feature regarding the tripled eyelid is that the coin examined shows a very strong die clash under the truncation of the bust at the rim, in front of Lincoln's bowtie and throat, and above the head near the motto. Little magnification is required to read the incuse, backward impression of the word PLURIBUS. Although die clashes are actually rather common on Lincoln cents, this one is especially strong. Die clashes that show outer lettering on the opposite face are rather scarce.

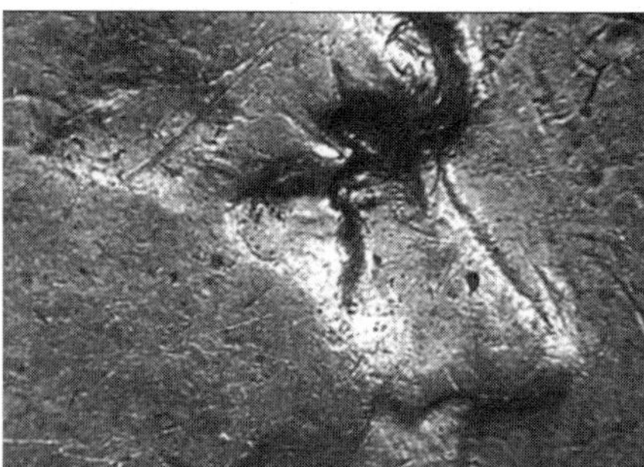

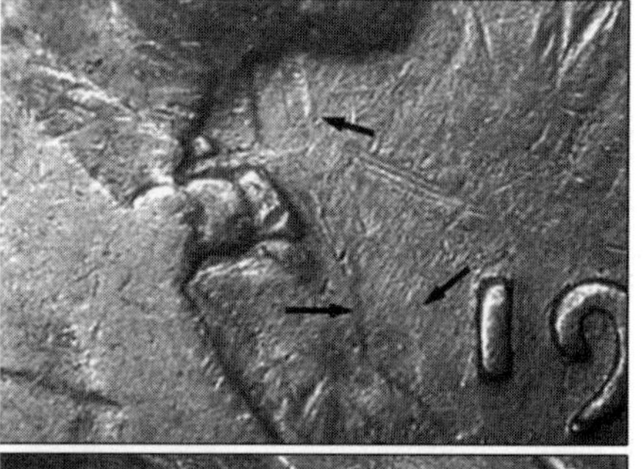

Photos of 1928P-1DO-001

Top: *The tripling shows as two separated upper eyelids to the south .*

Center: *Clash marks extend south from the lower beard and in front of the 1 of the date. These marks are produced by the central region of the letters of ONE CENT from the reverse.*

Bottom: *Think backward and upside down and you should be able to make out the IBU of PLURIBUS from the motto on the upper part of the reverse.*

Photos by author, coin from the Bob Piazza collection.

Right: *1928S-1MM-001 shows a tripled repunching to the north. This is the best defined RPM for this year. Photo by Bob Piazza.*

1929-1930

Production numbers increased from previous years, but the general rule regarding strike in the branch mints remains about the same. While many examples of Denver and San Francisco Mint issues for both of these years are somewhat indistinct, sharp examples from all mints can be found with modest effort. All issues from both dates are common in circulated grades.

Repunched mintmarks and doubled dies are on nearly equal levels for these two years, and are pretty much hit or miss. Most are not extravagant or difficult to find in circulated grades. However, as with other early years, they can be quite difficult to obtain in mint state.

This photo of 1929S-1MM-001 shows a north spread as an extra upper loop and upper serif to the north. It also shows the generally indistinct nature of the details that is extant on most early San Francisco minted cents, especially those of the mid to late 1920s. Photo by author.

1930S-1MM-001 looks much like 1929S-1MM-001. It shows an extra upper curve and upper serif to the north. Very light doubling can be seen inside and on the left edge of the D of GOD — this is master die doubling that shows on many examples of 1930-S cents. Although it is a form of hub doubling, it is not considered a doubled die. Photos by author.

1930P-1DR-001 shows class 6 distended hub doubling as strong extra thickness (toward the rim) of both wheat stalks, all lettering in the motto, and on the top half of the lettering in ONE. Doubled dies like this are known on earlier cents, but in 1930 this type of doubing becomes more prevelant. Photo by author.

1931

Considered one of the keys of the Lincoln cent series, the 1931-S cent receives most of the attention this year. Mintage figures numbering only 866,000 are the first under one million since the 1909-S V.D.B. variety and to date remain second in rarity among all business strike Lincoln cent issues.

Expectation that they would be valuable started early when mintage figures were released. Massive hoarding in the 1930's preserved many examples in uncirculated grades. However, storage techniques used in that era left many of the uncirculated coins spotted or discolored. For this reason, dipped and cleaned coins with uncirculated details are prevalent.

Circulated examples of 1931-S cents are actually less common than the uncirculated examples, thus the value difference among all grades has the lowest spread of all early Lincoln cents. According to the March, 2004 issue of *Coin Market*, a supplement of *Numismatic News*, 1931-S cents in G-4 condition value at $52.50 and those in MS-63 for $95.00, for a spread of only $42.50. In contrast, the difference in value for 1926-S cents between the same two grades is $197.00.

This value difference is not a recent occurrence. The 1970 edition of *A Guide Book of United States Coins*, values the 1931-S cent at $20.00 in Good and at $60.00 in Unc. The same guide lists the 1926-S at $2.75 in Good and $100.00 in Unc.

Beware of altered coins from other dates disguised as 1931-S cents. Because of their scarcity, they have been frequently counterfeited. The most common method of counterfeiting is by taking a genuine S mint cent from 1936 and pushing the shape of the 6 into a 1. The easiest way to discern these from genuine 1931-S cents is to observe the shape of the 3 in the date.

Few die varieties are known for this date. Fortunately for those on a budget, none of those reported are on 1931-S cents. A single example of class 6 distended hub doubling is known for 1931-P, and a single repunched mintmark has been reported for 1931-D. Photos were not available at the time this book was written, however, the 1931-D RPM has a northwest spread and is detectable under a 16 power loupe.

Comparison photo between normal 1931-S and 1936-S cents to show the difference in the shape of the 3 of the date. Notice how the top of the 3 on the 1931-S cent is more curved and is shorter than the bottom of the digit, while the top and bottom of the 3 on the 1936 cent are straighter and more symmetrical. Photos by author.

1932-1933

Mostly because the United States was in the middle of the Great Depression, 1932 and 1933 cents were among the lowest mintages of any year of Lincoln cent. 1932 marks the first year in cent history where branch mint production exceeded that of the main mint in Philadelphia (when the Philadelphia Mint actually made cents). Behind 1922, when only Denver minted cents, 1932 and 1933 are second and third as years with the lowest number of cents minted.

Both years have been sought after since their release and were never found regularly in circulation. Widespread hoarding of the coins that were available preserved a good deal of them in nicer grades. Though expensive, uncirculated specimens are still available.

Light master die doubling is visible underneath the upper part of the 32 of the date on this 1932 cent.

Neither year is very well known for die varieties. A 1932 doubled master die is the culprit in leaving a lot of observant collectors thinking they have something valuable when they find doubling in the date. This is common for coins from both mints and carries no premium value.

1933 has a couple of rather minor D mint RPMs and only one known doubled die. The doubled die is class 6 distended hub doubling, and is most visible as extra thickness in the date and the letters in TRUST, although less evident extra thickness is visible on all other obverse devices.

Observant collectors will also notice a change in the '3' digit(s) in the date between 1932 and 1933. No particular reason is known for the change, however the unique shape of the '3' digits on 1930-1932 cents help determine their authenticity, as was explained in the text for 1931.

1933D-1DO-001 shows mild class 6 distended hub doubling. Notice the extra thickness in the date and the concave shape at the top of the two letters "T" of TRUST. Photo by author.

1933D-1MM-002 shows a well defined repunched mintmark to the east.

MODERN WHEAT CENTS: 1934-1958

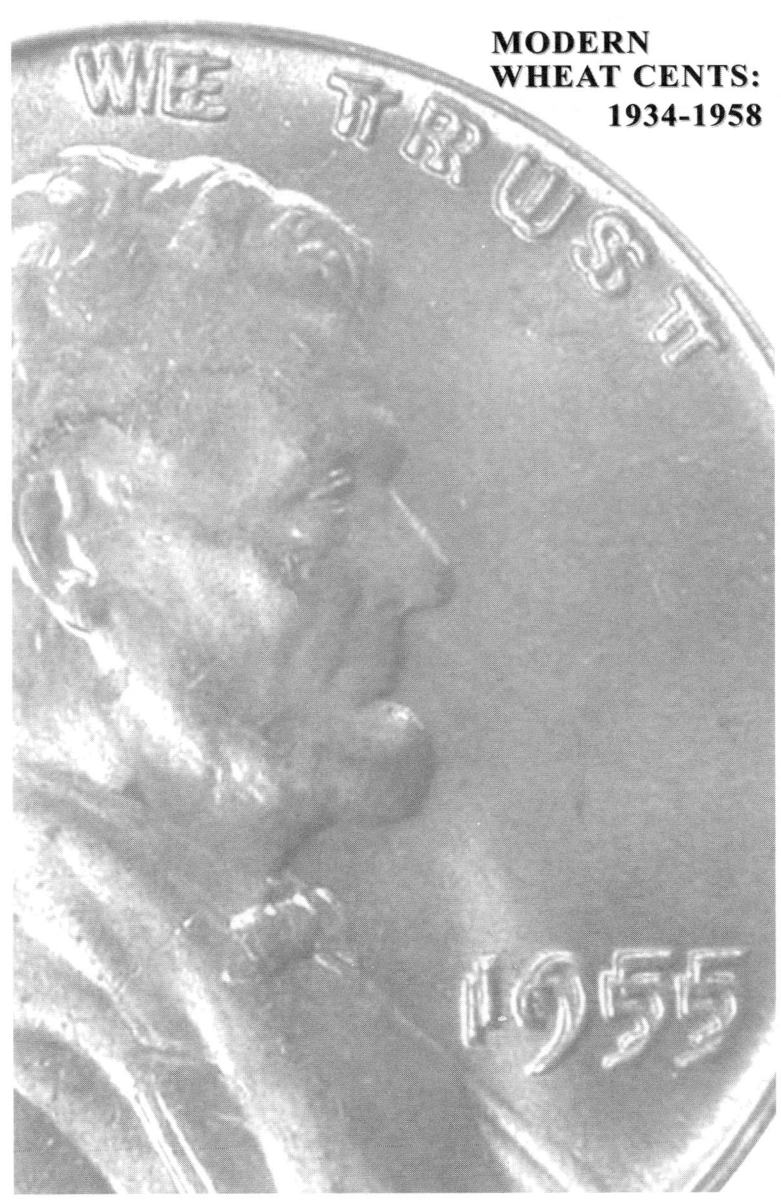

Overview

From the introduction of the Lincoln cent to 1934, the United States experienced World War I, a dust bowl, the Great Depression, and the administration of seven U.S. presidents. While many nations' coins went through nearly half a dozen changes per denomination, the lowly Lincoln cent was just getting started.

1934 marks the beginning of a new era in cent production. Up to that point, the U.S. Mint had produced just over 4 billion cents in 25 years — a mark that would only take another nine years to double. With the exception of 1934, production levels of cents in the new era never dropped to pre-1934 levels and, except in a handful of cases, steadily increased each year.

Large-scale hoarding began because of the newfound abundance of coins. By the end modern wheat cents era, economic prosperity, brought on by victory in World War II, allowed anyone who wanted to save cents the ability to do so. Tens of thousands of bags worth of mint-fresh cents were saved during this period, creating an abundance of shiny red mint state cents that is still extant today.

Over 21 billion cents were minted in the era of the modern wheat cent, yet more unique rarities were minted in the 25 years it encompasses than in any other era of the Lincoln cent. It was during this era that collectors began to realize there was more to the rarity of a coin than the number minted. The discovery of 1955 cents exhibiting doubled designs marked the beginning of a sub-variety of numismatists who studied each coin closely and cataloged those that were anomalous.

Although the "error and variety" market is stronger today than it has ever been, we owe its beginning to the Lincoln cent and the era of the modern wheat cent.

1934

Even though cents were produced at only two facilities this year, (Philadelphia and Denver) production was higher than the past three years combined. Philadelphia Mint 1934 cents are widely available in mint state grades and are plentiful even in higher grades. Today, Denver Mint 1934 cents are not quite as available in high grades because quality control at the Denver Mint still had not reached the level of the Philadelphia Mint. Circulated rolls of both are available and are inexpensive compared to years past.

For these reasons, 1934 is considered the first year of widely available and affordable Lincoln cents, and marks the first year of what most consider "modern wheat cents." Many collectors, even those on a budget, tend to start adding uncirculated grades to their sets beginning with the 1934 cent.

Although mintage of the cent increased greatly in 1934, the number of known die varieties stayed rather level. Only a handful of known die varieties are worth mentioning.

Another oddity of note is that the 3 digit in the year of 1934 cents differs from that of 1933 and 1932. It points downward at the bottom and is thicker than the previous two years. The same shape of 3 in the date would not be seen again until 1943.

This year also marked a sad note in the history of the Lincoln cent. Its designer, Victor David Brenner, passed away at the age of 52.

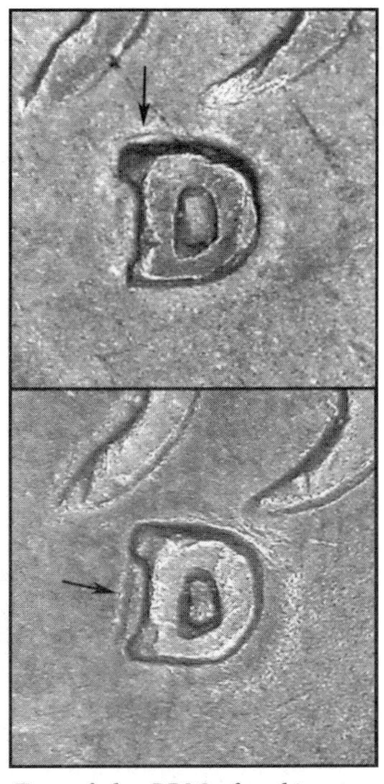

Two of the RPMs for this year. These are 1934D-1MM-001 and 1934D-1MM-002 respectively. Photos by Bob Piazza.

Above: *1934D-1DO-001 shows distended hub doubling (class 6) which is common for this era.* **Below**: *1934P-1DO-001 and 1934P-1DR-001, two class 6 doubled dies in the same die pairing. Photos by author.*

These photos show an unfortunately cleaned example of a very rare doubled die. 1934P-1DO-002 shows a completely separated date to the southeast of the primary date. The top photo shows the coin in its natural state with arrows pointing to the extra digits, while the bottom photo shows the same area with digital overlay enhancement to better depict the placement of the errant date. This doubled die is the only known example of its particular type in the Lincoln cent series and commands a very high premium value. In Very Fine, this coin would be worth in excess of $75. In About Uncirculated the same die is worth $200 or more. Photos by author.

These two coins were minted with the same die, but are of differing die states. They are both 1934D-1MM-002, and are shown here together to illustrate the importance of die state when collecting die varieties. Which of these would you rather own? Photos by author.

1935

This is the earliest year of the Lincoln cent in which uncirculated specimens are readily available and affordable in modest grades, and rolls of all three mints are rather abundant. Although many branch mint cents still lack in overall die quality, the general rule is that all three mints are available and can be found with minimal effort in sharp detail and with higher grades. Circulated rolls are very common and quite inexpensive.

Partly because affordability makes this issue readily available to most collectors, a number of die varieties are known for this date, the majority of which are doubled dies. Because many different class 6 distended hub doubled dies are known for this year and the decade that follows, it is believed that there was a problem in die production that took some time to solve.

A very common oddity to watch for this year that carries no premium value is a circular depression inside the

This 1935 cent shows an oddity which is common for the date on all three mint's issues. The ridge that connects the end of the bottom loop of the 5 with the top half of the 5 appears to have come from the plaster mold that created master dies for the year. Photo by author.

lower portion of the 5 of the date. This must have occurred on a master die used indirectly to create dies for all three mints, since this anomaly is found on coins from all three mints. It is not a doubled die or misplaced mintmark, as some have reported.

1935P-1DO-001 has proven to be a very elusive yet very nice doubled die. It is a class 5, pivoted hub doubled die with a clockwise pivot from the 9 o'clock position (as looking on a clock face). What this ends up producing is nice doubling on the word TRUST and the date, and no doubling at all visible on LIBERTY. Photos by author.

This year marks the first of many in which class 6 doubled dies such as the one photographed here become common. This is 1935P-1DR-001, a very strong example of this class of doubling. Notice the doubling on both wheat stalks, the motto, and the top of ONE. Photos by author.

1936

Very high mintage numbers from all three mints, combined with the massive hoarding of rolled coins, makes this date readily available in all grades. For the first time since the teens, the branch mint coins tend to be of roughly the same quality as Philadelphia Mint strikes; however, lower quality coins minted from problematic dies do remain.

This year marks the reintroduction of the proof cent, the first such issue since 1916. The Mint began striking satin proofs early in the year, but because of customer complaints it switched later in the year to minting brilliant proofs. Both types are very scarce, with just over 5,000 total pieces minted. The satin proof is 4 times scarcer than the brilliant proof, although it sells for less because it is less popular with collectors.

The dies varieties of this year are highly sought after by collectors. 1936 boasts the highest number of major doubled dies in the Lincoln cent series. While 1955 and 1972 show stronger doubling on one single die than any produced in 1936, the number of faintly naked-eye doubled dies for 1936 is more than double that of any other year.

Machine doubling is very prevelant on 1936 cents. Notice the lack of notching at the corners of the 36 on this coin. Photo by Bob Piazza.

Doubled dies on the reverse of all mints of 1936 cents are prolific this year. Mainly consisting of class 6 distended hub doubled dies, these coins are both fun to look for and a challenge to properly attribute because of the sheer number of different dies that exhibit the doubling. At the time of this writing, over a dozen different 1936-P, D, and S doubled die reverses are known. Be careful when trying to self-attribute these doubled dies, as many of them are very similar in appearance.

Watch for machine doubling on this year's cents, as it seems to be more prevalent than in surrounding years. Especially found on the obverse, this common anomaly is a very unwelcome problem for a year that has so many doubled dies. Not only do they fool many a novice into thinking they have a valuable coin, but they annoy experienced die variety hunters when they find a nice doubled die that also shows

Notice on this example of 1936P-1DO-001 that in one of the two hubbings that caused the doubling the lower left leg of the R is broken off. Photo by Bob Piazza

machine doubling. Seen as a distraction by die variety hunters, machine doubling can affect the value of doubled dies and repunched mintmarks.

An example of an odd die anomaly that shows on many 1936 cents is a broken R in LIBERTY. These provide an interesting curiosity but are quite common and do not warrant a premium value unto themselves.

Four different doubled die obverses found on 1936P cents. In order, 1936P-1DO-001, 002, 003, and 004. Photos by Bob Piazza.

1936P-1DO-001 shows very nice doubling in all areas of the design. This doubled die is somewhat scarce, but used to be rather easy to locate in mixed bags of wheat cents. Since being listed in major guides a decade ago, it has become increasingly difficult to cherrypick. Note the clear separation to the southwest on all devices on the coin. This is indicative of a class 4, offset hub doubled die. Photos by Bob Piazza.

1936P-1DO-002 shows stronger doubling in the date and the latter half of LIBERTY on circulated coins, and shows some light doubling in the motto on higher grade coins. This is because this die is actually a tripled die. The second hubbing was offset to the southwest and the third hubbing was tilted and rotated slightly clockwise creating a class 4 + 8 hub tripled die.

One of the markers of this die is the broken left leg of the R of LIBERTY in the second hubbing. This is evident even on this circulated specimen — the left leg of the R is of normal thickness while the rest of the latter half of LIBERTY is very thick indicating the doubling. Photos by Bob Piazza.

1936P-1DO-003 shows class 5 pivoted hub doubling in the motto and LIBERTY on lower grade specimens (as photographed here) and lighter doubling on the date and bust on higher grade coins. The doubling was pivoted at a point near the rim under the date. Because the date does not show much doubling on this die, its value is substantially lower than that of dies #1 and #2. It sells for $40-$80 in typical circulated grades. Photos by Bob Piazza.

1936P-1DR-001 displays a common thread among many of the class 6 distended hub doubled die reverse of this era. An egg-shaped dot in the motto is the main pick up point in the spread. Notice that because this example is late die state the doubling does not show very well in UNUM or on the right wheat stalk. Photos by author.

1936D-1DR-001 is somewhat stronger than its P mint counterpart. Notice that the tip of the wheat lines does not come to a sharp point as it should, and that the outer edge is void of the lines. This is part of the doubling, and in some cases, as with this one, it extends all the way down the wheat stalks to the stems. Photos by author.

1937

Yet another bumper crop of cents was minted this year. Philadelphia mintage dropped very slightly from 1936 levels, but mintage at both branch mints picked up by roughly 10 million cents per mint. Cents from all mints can be found with crisp detail and gorgeous color. However, these features are still somewhat more common on Philadelphia minted examples.

Proof cents make yet another appearance this year — nearly twice as many were minted this year as last. These proofs are available, yet rather expensive for low-budget collectors. All proofs minted this year and all remaining years of the Lincoln cent are brilliant proof.

Doubled dies are the rule once again for die variety hunters. Although they do not have the charm (or spread) of the 1936 doubled dies, many class 2 and class 6 doubled die obverses have been reported from all mints. As in 1936, many doubled die reverses, mainly class 6, are also known to exist.

1937 has a case of master die doubling that confuses a number of collectors. Light doubling is visible on the 7 of the date on about half of the coins minted. A photo is provided to help you discern this from valuable hub doubling.

The thin bar of doubling seen on the 7 in this photo is master doubling that shows on many 1937 cents. Photo by author.

Repunched mintmarks are not as evident as with some other years, although a few do exist. None of the known RPMs are very strong, nor are any of them exceedingly scarce.

1937P-1DO-001 shows light to moderate class 2 distorted hub doubling toward the center of the design on the date and motto. This doubled die should not be mistaken for the common master die doubling shown on the previous page. The master die doubling does not show doubling this clearly in the motto. Photos by author.

1937P-1DR-002 shows the most extreme class 6 distended hub doubling spread of any wheat cent reported to coppercoins.com. All of the lettering and other devices near the rim have nearly four times the thickness of a normal cent. Notice how even the wheat stalks near the lower reverse are extremely thick. Coin reported by Frank Baumann, photos by author.

1937P-1DR-001P shows a very nice early proof Lincoln cent doubled die. This die is extremely scarce in that not only is it a proof coin with a total mintage of fewer than 10,000 coins, but is also only one representative die of likely five or six different dies used to mint all 1937 proof cents. This along with the theory that relatively few of the minted coins are still in collectible condition gives us the idea that there are few of these gems remaining in collectors' hands. This particular die sells for $300-$500 in typical proof grades, with examples exhibiting cameo frost selling for far more.

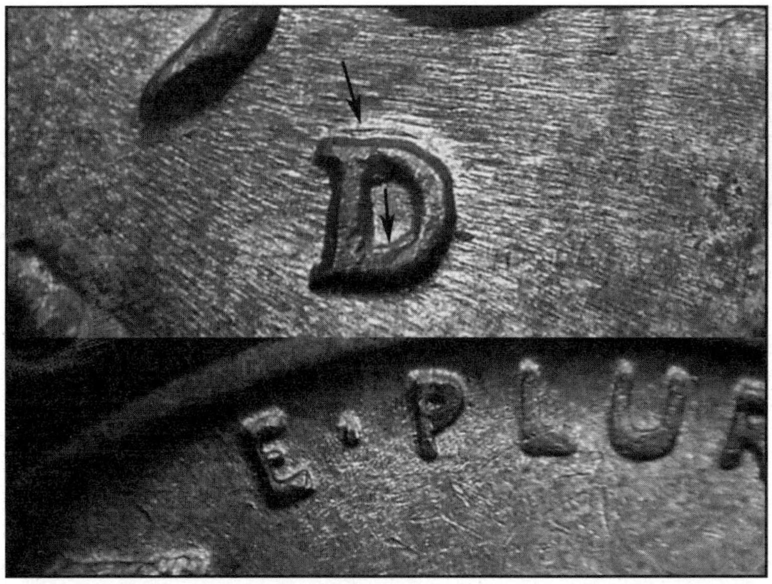

11937D-1MM-001 is a rather nice repunched mintmark with a north spread. It packs a double whammy, though — it is also a doubled die, 1937D-1DR-001. Photos by author.

1937D-1DO-001 shows class 6 doubling in the date and LIBERTY along with class 5 doubling in LIBERTY, the motto and on the 7 of the date. With two classes of hub doubling, this is a tripled die. Photos by author.

1937S-1DO-002 shows class 6 distended hub doubling that is common for San Francisco minted obverses for this year. Notice the extra thickness in the date, motto, and LIBERTY. It is likely that most, if not all of the S mint doubled dies like this one, were created with the same working hub.

1938

Cent production declined this year for the first time since 1931 but the overall impact was slight. Although production was nearly half that of the year before, 1938 cents from all mints are readily available in uncirculated rolls, and circulated examples are inexpensive and easy to find. Even the values of the single coins are unaffected by the lower mintage into uncirculated grades.

1938 marks the first year for which more than ten thousand proof cents were minted. Prices reflect this in that 1938 proof cents still sell for under $100 in many cases, making it the earliest proof cent that sells at these levels.

Repunched mintmarks tend to define this year's die varieties, primarily because they are relatively easy to find. They tend to be more common than any RPM issued to date and are more common than any yet to be issued through 1943. At least six different RPMs are known for the Denver Mint cents, while three are known for the San Francisco minted cents.

Doubled dies are still quite common on 1938 cents, but do not get the attention given to the year's RPMs. Class 6 doubled die reverses are still the prevalent rule for 1938 cents. More than half a dozen different examples are known between the three mints.

Master die doubling that shows as doubling to the south on the 8 of the date is very common this year for all three mints. Because it is master die doubling, it warrants no premium value even though it is a form of hub doubling just like doubled dies.

An example of the master die doubling that shows on many 1938 cents. Notice the doubling to the south inside and on the bottom of the digit. Photo by author.

Machine doubling is prevalent among this year's cents as well, especially on the obverse. Quite a number of 1938 cents have been reported and turned down as doubled die obverses for this reason.

1938S-1MM-001, 002, and 003 respectively. These repunched mintmarks, while nice, are found commonly in 1938-S rolls. Oddly enough the nicest looking of the three, 1938S-1MM-002, is the most common while the most minor of the three, 1938S-1MM-003, is the hardest of the three to find. Photos by author.

Two of the more common repunched mintmarks for 1938-D cents are 1938D-1MM-002 (left) and 1938D-1MM-005 (right). At some point during the process of minting 1938D-1MM-002 the reverse die was changed to a class 6 doubled die. Photos by author.

One of the nicer doubled die reverses for this year is 1938P-1DR-001. Like many others of this era, this die exhibits class 6 hub doubling, but notice that instead of just extra thickness in the wheat stems, there is also clear separation. This adds class 2, distorted hub doubling to the die, making this a multiple class doubled die. It is a class 2 + 6 doubled die. Photos by author.

1939

Mintage is up once again to 1937 levels for the Philadelphia and San Francisco Mints. However, Denver Mint production is at its lowest in five years. Rolls from all three mints were heavily hoarded, so they are still available at reasonably affordable prices. Quality tends to be a problem once again for San Francisco; many survivors are spotty with soft details.

Repunched mintmarks are on the low side this year. Only five different RPMs are known between both branch mints, and only one of those is strong enough to easily see with a low power grading loupe.

Doubled dies are on the rise this year. While most are of the same basic type as with the past four years, one stands out as being very different. It is a very strongly spread class 1 rotated hub doubled die with a very weak first hubbing. If you are only looking at the outer devices on the obverse of P mint cents, you will miss this one. It only shows doubling on the ERTY of LIBERTY, the 19 of the date, and on Lincoln's bowtie and eye. Other doubled dies for this year number over a dozen, so watch for them closely. Almost all of them are class 6 distended hub doubled dies.

1939D-1MM-001 is a strong D/D north RPM. It is one of only two known for the Denver mint this year. Photo by author.

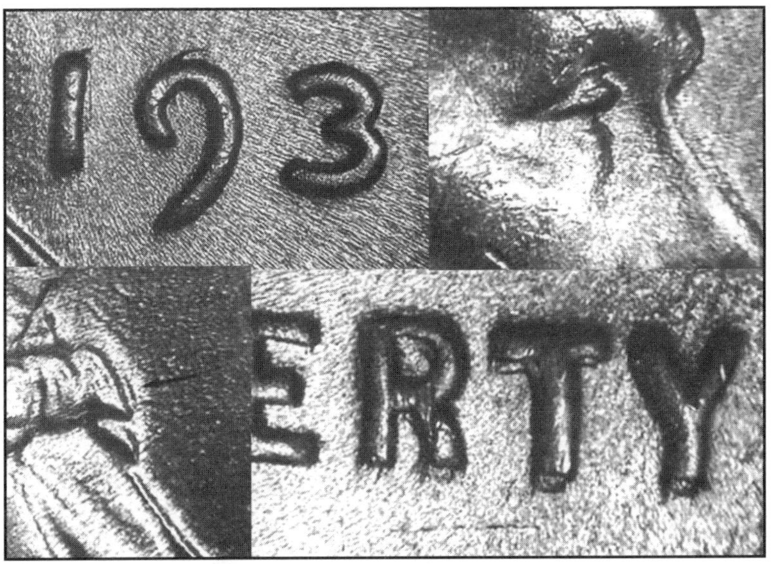

1939P-1DO-001 shows doubling on the 19 of the date, on Lincoln's eyelid and bowtie, and in the RTY of LIBERTY. Photos by author.

1939S-1MM-002 shows a very nice spread to the north. It is one of the nicer RPMs for the era and is quite scarce in uncirculated grades. Photo by author.

1940

This date begins a period in cent production that sets new records. The Philadelphia and Denver Mints produced more cents this year than in any other year to date, and San Francisco was not far behind their record. Original uncirculated rolls are still available for all mints, and circulated coins from this date are very common.

The proof mintage, while low compared to that of more modern proofs, exceeded any proof mintage of Lincoln cents to date. Over 15,000 pieces were struck. They are still readily available in a wide range of grades and are priced from around $70 and up, depending on grade.

1940 presents die variety hunters with a nice challenge. With over two dozen known doubled dies and over a dozen known repunched mintmarks for all three mints, this year presents a wonderful array of nice treasures to find.

Class 6 doubled die reverses still rule this year. A large number of coins have been found representing over a dozen different dies. Class 6 obverses are also prevalent.

Denver minted repunched mintmarks are a bit easier to find than their San Francisco counterparts, but with some diligence, none of the repunched mintmarks for this year are exceedingly difficult to obtain through dealer stock, circulated rolls, or even uncirculated rolls.

Master die doubling as seen on the 40 of the date on many 1940 cents. Photo by author.

Master die doubling occurs on the last two digits of the date this year. Very light doubling is visible on the outer right edge and inside left edge of the 0, and on the right edge and end of the crosslet in the 4. No premium value is warranted for such doubling this year, as it is very common.

While on the subject of the 4 of the date, note that there are serifs not only on the bottom of the digit but also vertical serifs at the end of the crosslet. This is unique to 1940, but all 1940 cents have this particular shape to the 4. It has been published that there are two different types of dates for 1940 cents, but this is incorrect.

Another common anomaly for this year is machine doubling, especially on the obverse of the coins. A number of these have been reported as hopeful candidates for doubled dies. Notice in the example below that not only is the 9 in the date shelf-doubled, but the mintmark is as well. This is a telling sign of machine doubling because the mintmark and date were added to the die in different processes at different times. It makes no logical sense that they would be doubled together except at the time the coin was minted — hence machine doubling.

Machine doubling on a 1940-S cent. Notice that the 9 and mintmark are both doubled in the same manner. Most cases with doubling in the date AND mintmark are machine doubling. Photo by Bob Piazza.

1940P-1DR-001 shows very strong class 2 and class 5 doubling on the reverse. Notice how not only is the doubling spread toward the center of the design, but is pivoted counterclockwise as well. Also notice that the right corners of the E of ONE are also notched. Photos by author.

1940D-1MM-002 is one of the more common repunched mintmarks for this date. It has a nice north spread that shows much better in earlier die states than does this late die state example. The reason for showing this coin, however is to illustrate two points; first, this is the more common die state people are likely to find this die in, and second, because this is a late die state coin, it shows that many were produced. Photo by author.

1940S-1MM-007 is one of the tougher repunched mintmarks to locate for this date. It shows a tripled spread, S/S/S east and east. Repunched mintmarks for 1940-S are generally a little tougher to locate than the Denver minted specimens. Photo by author.

1940S-1MM-001 presents us with an interesting double whammy in the form of a doubled die obverse, 1940S-1DO-001. The repunched mintmark shows as a nice S/S northeast, while the doubled die is class 6 distended hub doubling, showing mainly in the 9 of the date, TRUST, and the first three letters of LIBERTY. This die is rather scarce in uncirculated grades. Photos by author.

1941

While Europe was in the early stages of World War II and Japan was planning its attack against the U.S. in the Pacific, the Mint was busy turning out record numbers of cents. Once again breaking the record set in the previous year, the three mints produced a combined 1.1 billion cents, marking the first time the Mint produced over 1 billion coins of a single denomination in any given year.

With this in mind, uncirculated rolls are rather plentiful, with Philadelphia Mint rolls commonly selling for under $75. Uncirculated singles for all three mints can be found in a wide range of grades, including MS-66 and MS-67, for much lower prices than in previous years. Circulated coins for this year and all following years are very common and no longer warrant mention.

Die varieties are widespread this year, with over three dozen different dies known altogether. Doubled die reverses, especially the typical class 6 reverses, are rather common. Other more interesting doubled dies are numerous, although difficult to locate and quite valuable.

San Francisco minted coins bear two different sizes of mintmarks this year. Like with 1928-S cents, the large mintmark is scarcer than the small mintmark. Unlike the 1928-S cent, there is little value

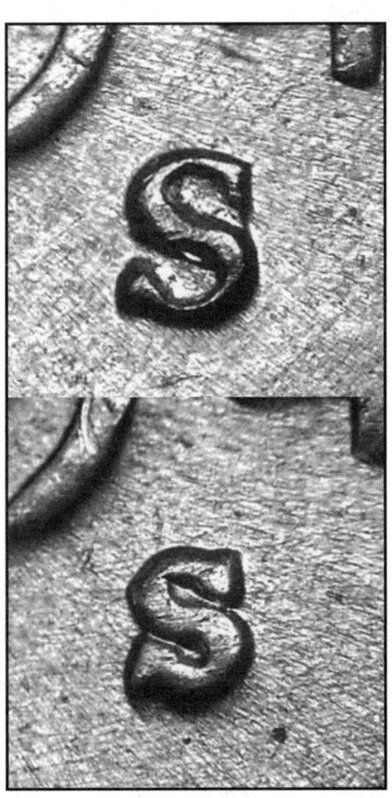

The two sizes of 1941-S mintmarks are very distinctly different. At top is the large mintmark, and at botton, the small mintmark. Photos by author.

difference between the two because generalist collectors have yet to realize the relational scarcity of the large to small, which in my experience examining them over a number of years, is approximately 1 to 12.

As with 1940 cents, 1941 cents also sport their share of machine doubling. Rather common, especially for Philadelphia minted cents on the obverse, these have been reported and rejected as doubled dies a number of times.

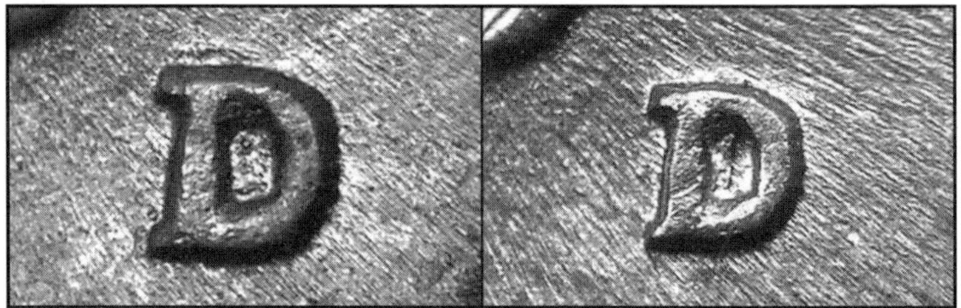

1941D-1MM-001 and 1941D-1MM-002. Although the repunched mintmarks for 1941-D cents are rather bland, they are among the toughest RPMs to locate for wheat cents, thus their values are quite high. Photos by author.

1941S-1DO-001 shows nice class 6 doubling. Photos by author.

While looking through your cents if you happen to find a repunched mintmark, do not forget that there is another side to the coin that could exhibit a doubled die—as is the case with this pair of die varieties. This is 1941D-1MM-007 and 1941D-1DR-003. Two different die varieties on the same coin. Photos by author.

1941D-1DR-002 shows a classic and typical example of class 6 doubling for this era. There are many doubled die reverses that are similar to this one for this date, so be careful when attributing them yourself. Photos by author.

1941P-1DO-001 shows a weakly hubbed but very wide spread in the motto, and also shows some doubling in the date and LIBERTY. This doubled die is quite scarce and is worth a hefty premium in higher grades. This is one example that shows why hubbing the dies a number of times was necessary. The design was never completely impressed into the die on the first pass through the hubbing press. Photos by Bob Piazza.

1941P-1DO-006 shows a strongly doubled ear, and a weak hubbing but very wide spread doubling on the TY of LIBERTY and the 19 of the date. Coins from this die are scarce in circulated grades and very rare in uncirculated grades. One reason for this is because many people only check their coins for hub doubling around the outside devices, and this doubled die would be missed under such examination. Photos by Bob Piazza.

1942

Overall cent production dropped this year because of the war — not because of a shortage of work force, but because the metals used to mint the coins were needed for the war effort. The Mint did what it could to conserve, especially when it came to copper. Tests were conducted in a number of different alloys, even wood and plastic, in an effort to make a good substitute coin for the mainly copper cent. More on this subject will follow with the 1943 text.

San Francisco mintage dropped only slightly from 1941 levels, but not enough to greatly affect their availability. Full uncirculated rolls are still available but command very high prices because they are touted as one of the keys to the modern Lincoln wheat cent subseries; they have for years been considered an investment level coin in uncirculated grades because their lack of quality usually precludes the superb gem grades. Circulated examples of 1942-S cents are common in all grades.

Die variety hunters will find this year to be exciting. Many doubled dies and repunched mintmarks are known for 1942 cents and a number of them are very nice and quite valuable. Although at least somewhat available in earlier years, the "doubled eye" class 4 doubled die makes a full-blown appearance for the first time this year. At least two strong doubled dies involving the eye and central part of the design are known this year.

1942D-1MM-002 and 1942D-1MM-003 are two of the RPMs to look for on this year's cents. Photos by author.

Repunched mintmarks abound this year, with a total of over two dozen from Denver and San Francisco combined. One of the more noteworthy repunched mintmarks this year is a wide spread to the south on an S mint die that also shows a nice doubled die.

1942P-1DO-001 shows light class 5 doubling on the lower part of the letters in LIBERTY and on IN GOD WE of the motto. This die is considered rare in all grades. Photos by Bob Piazza.

Above*: 1942P-1DO-002 shows strong doubling on Lincoln's profie and eye, and weaker doubling on the 19 of the date.*

Top Right*: Another class 4 doubled die, 1942P-1DO-003 shows doubling on Lincoln's eye and the first T of TRUST (next page).*

Lower Right*: 1942S-1MM-001 shows a very wide spread to the south. What is particularly interesting about this die is that it is also a rather nice doubled die obverse, showing mainly on the tops of the letters in LIBERTY and on top of the 9 of the date, but also shows inside Lincoln's ear and above his eyelid. This die is rather scarce in higher grades (next page).*

1943

This year is probably the most interesting year of all Lincoln cents for many collectors. An alloy change took place this year because the copper used in cent production was needed for the production of ammunition used in World War II. Tests were conducted during the last half of 1942 to find a suitable substitute for copper. After trying different metals and other non-metallic materials such as clay, plastic, and wood, the Mint settled on steel plated zinc for 1943 cents.

Despite patriotism and support for the war effort, the general public disliked the new coin. Many reports surfaced by mid-1943 claiming that the coin was often confused with and used as a dime. An article in the October 04, 1943 issue of the Troy, New York, *Troy Record*, reported that Mint Director Ross had tried a number of times in failure to change the color of the new cents to brown because of the public contempt for their color.

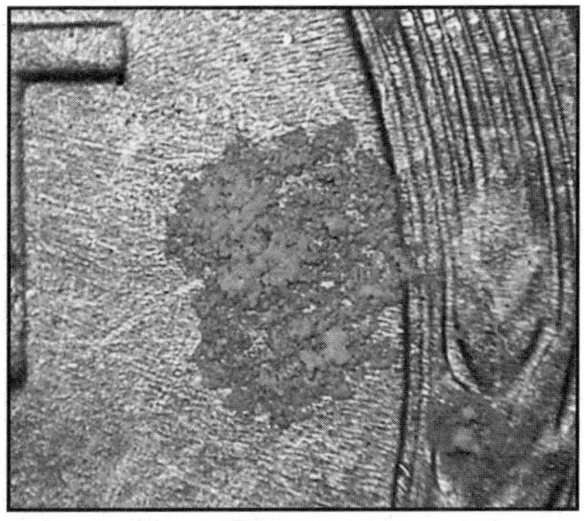

Above: *Zinc oxide corrosion.*

Below: *A rusted 1943 cent.*

Other attempts included punching a hole through the center of the coins to more easily distinguish them from dimes, but that experiment ended in failure as well because the coins would not register in vending machines.

This retained CUD is on the reverse of a 1943-S cent. It will break off into a full CUD before the die is retired.

Mintage was up only slightly in Philadelphia and Denver, but nearly doubled in San Francisco, with overall production once again exceeding the one billion mark set in 1941. The increase in production, coupled with the fact that 1943 cents are so different from other years, led to widespread hoarding by the public. Today, uncirculated examples, even in gem condition, are very common for all three mints. Uncirculated rolls are commonplace and mint state singles are easy to obtain for under $5 each.

The steel and zinc composition, in hindsight, was chosen in poor judgment. Steel and zinc are both reactive metals to the oxygen in air and water. When exposed to the common environmental conditions to which coins are typically subjected, steel rusts (ferrous oxide) and zinc turns into zinc oxide, a powdery white substance. 1943 cents, even gem specimens, are always at risk of such chemical reactions. A large number of singles and rolls that were hoarded have been ruined by

Abraded die doubling (arrows) is most common on the 4 of the date and the mintmark on 1943 cents, although it is quite common and possible on other areas of the coin. Photo by Bob Piazza.

simple exposure to air and moisture during storage. One solution to help protect examples that remain undamaged is to use a swab to lightly coat the steel cent with pure mineral oil. If done properly, this will provide some protection for the coins. Unfortunately, once damaged by rust, 1943 cents are irreparable.

Another reason steel was a poor choice for cents is that it is much harder than copper based alloys, and thus more difficult to mint. This is evidenced by a large number of coins with die cracks and breaks. Because the pressure and spacing between the dies were adjusted to compensate for the harder metal, die clashes are also very common.

Also, because of the adjustments necessary to strike the steel cents, worn dies were another major problem. A vast number of cents were minted with severely worn dies that exhibit characteristics quite unlike the wear found on bronze cents. Many times, the wear will be centralized to areas around the mintmark and the date, causing heavy

A 1943-S cent with a nearly missing mintmark. These are common this year. Photo by Bob Piazza.

abraded die doubling on these devices. Novice die variety hunters frequently find these coins and misidentify them as repunched mintmarks or doubled dies.

Another problem exhibited by the extremely worn dies was flattened devices, usually the 4 digit in the date and the mintmark. They often appear repressed and shiny, or thicker and lower in relief, than they would otherwise normally appear. There have also been a number of cases reported in which these

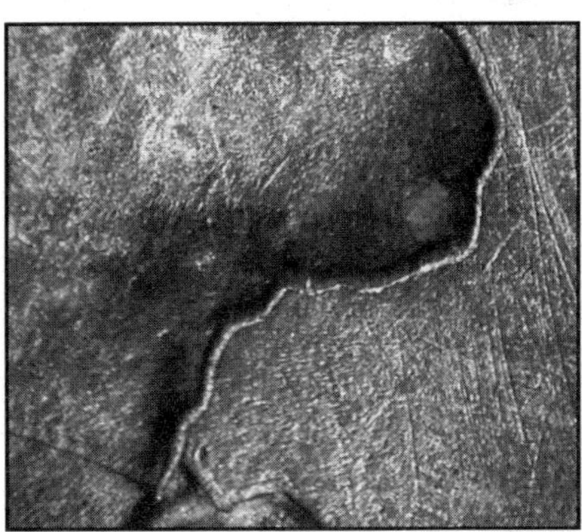

A slightly recessed trench is visible along the entire outline of Lincoln's bust on this cent. Although sporadically evident in other years' cents, these are most common this year. Photo by author.

devices were nearly invisible. When these catch the eye of unknowing generalist collectors and dealers, they are touted as valuable errors. In fact, they are very common and warrant no premium value.

Because the dies had a tendency to wear out quickly, measures were taken to prolong the life of the design by engraving a trench around Lincoln's bust (to enhance the outline) on the hubs used to make the dies. This design enhancement transposes to the coins as a recessed trench around the bust. Because this is extremely common, it should be ignored as a part of the design. Most 1943 cents exhibit this trench; it has been reported as hub doubling on a number of occasions.

As for true die varieties, 1943 exhibits a number of doubled dies and repunched mintmarks, although many of them are minor. As with the last few years, watch both sides of the coins for class 2 and class 6 hub doubling. Another heavily reported classification of doubling,

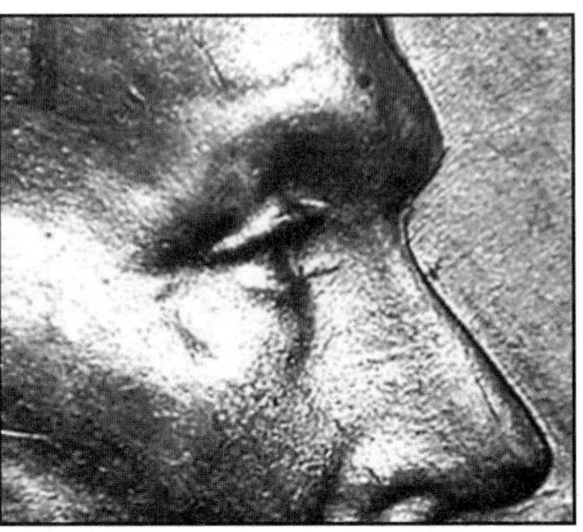

1943D-1DO-002: one of many 1943 "doubled eyelid" doubled dies. Photo by author.

like with 1942 cents, is class 4 offset hub doubling in the form of a doubled eye. Many true hub double dies exist, such as the "doubled eyelid." Unfortunately, they are both minor and common, and therefore of no particular value. Other class 4 doubled dies show heavier doubling in the eye area and on the date. These are easier to spot and are quite valuable in uncirculated grades.

1943D-1MM-001 is one of the nicest repunched mintmarks in the Lincoln cent series. Coin by Doug Yost.

For the mintmark variety collectors, watch for any of the nearly two-dozen known repunched mintmarks, which can be very difficult to detect on coins minted with the aforementioned worn dies. One of the D minted repunched mintmarks has a very wide spread to the southwest and is extremely valuable in uncirculated grades. In fact, because of the nature of the problems experienced while minting the steel cents, most of the individual dies had a much shorter life span than those of other years. As such, quite a few of the doubled dies and repunched mintmarks for this year are scarcer than in surrounding years. Because

The coin on the left is a typical uncirculated 1943 cent. Notice the satiny brilliant finish. The coin on the right is a reprocessed 1943 cent. Notice that it has lost all of its luster in lieu of a chrome-like sheen. Also notice that the details on the reprocessed cent are thicker than normal. Photos by author.

they are not only scarcer but are also different from other years of cents, 1943 die varieties tend to carry a higher premium than that of other years in the 1940's.

Because steel cents corroded and rusted very easily, it has become common practice for private businesses to purchase rolls and bags of lightly circulated or rusted cents at very low prices, brush off the corrosion or rust, and re-coat the coins with zinc. These "reprocessed" cents have no numismatic value and should be avoided by collectors buying coins for value. Often sold in sets as reprocessed cents, they are also commonly offered and purchased as uncirculated 1943 cents at uncirculated prices. They are easy to detect because the luster that would be apparent on a normal 1943 cent is gone, and the entire coin takes on a more chrome-like appearance. In addition, examination with low-power magnification will reveal bubbles in the coating and a general but slight loss of detail.

Last but not least, and certainly worth mention, are the "copper" (actually bronze) 1943 cents minted this year. Accidental in nature, some examples of 1943 cents were minted on bronze planchets probably intended for 1942 cents. Although less than two-dozen are known from all mints, these coins receive much more attention when discovered than do most other anomalies in the Lincoln cent series. For this reason, they are very heavily counterfeited.

The most common method of counterfeiting 1943 bronze cents involves plating a normal 1943 cent with copper. These counterfeits are very easily detected by holding the coin close to a magnet. 1943 cents were minted in magnetic steel. Unlike cents minted on bronze planchets, a copper plated steel cent will stick to the magnet. Fewer than five percent of the reported bronze 1943 cents pass this test. All of those fail the next test.

The second most common form of counterfeiting bronze 1943 cents is to shave off the left half of the 8 on a normal 1948 cent. Because 1948 cents are bronze, they do not stick to a magnet, thus passing the magnet test. Where they fail is in the shape of the digits of the date. Because the shape of the 3 used in 1943 is unique to 1934 and 1943, the shape of the 3 on a carved 1948 cent looks nothing like the genuine 1943 cent, as illustrated in the photos.

A genuine 1943 cent is shown on the top compared to a digitally enhanced 1948 cent with the 8 transformed into a 3. This example is much better than carved 1948 cents, and even at that the shape of the 3 is quite far off of the genuine 1943 cent. Photos by author.

Realistically, finding a genuine bronze 1943 cent in this day and age would be a very unlikely event. Occasionally, a local TV station will run a story reporting that a bronze 1943 cent has surfaced. The fact is that all known specimens are accounted for and are certainly not circulating in the locations reported from on the news. When you come across a bronze 1943 cent, the overwhelming odds are that it's a counterfeit.

Two of the doubled die obverses for 1943-D involving the date. This is 1943D-1DO-001 (top) and 1943D-1DO-003 (bottom). Notice that the 1 and 9 are doubled on both coins. 1943D-1DO-001 also comes with an RPM, 1943D-1MM-016, a minor example of a D/D south repunched mintmark. Photos by author.

1943S-1DR-001 shows class 6 doubling that is still widespread as with previous dates. Notice that on this example the doubling is stronger on the right side of the design, especially evident in the wheat stems. Photos by author.

1944

Another record is broken as mintage soars to unprecedented levels during this year. For the first time in U.S. history, a single mint coins more than one billion examples of any denomination for any year. Coinage demands by the American public and the general failure of the 1943 steel cents causes a 24 hour-a-day need to produce cents.

Mintage is higher than ever at both branch mints as well. Denver minted 217.6 million coins and San Francisco minted just over 191.5 million coins. This increase in production came with a price: many 1944 cents show at least modest die fatigue, especially on the reverse. Finding very well struck, full detail examples of 1944 branch mint cents is not rare by any means, but it is somewhat unusual.

1944 is the first year for what has become known as "shellcase bronze" cents. A surplus in spent shell casings from World War II battles, combined with the general failure of steel cents, persuaded the Mint to revert back to a copper based composition for the cents. The Mint acquired the metal for this change from shell casings — mainly the larger cannon shells from naval and artillery units. There is little difference in composition between 1942 and 1944 cents. However, the 1944 cents tend to change color over time to a more brassy-orange color than the earlier coinage. This is typically attributed to the sulphur in the powder used to discharge the projectiles in the shells. The "shellcase bronze" cents were minted through 1947.

The die varieties for 1944 can be summed up with one word — fantastic! Two nice over mintmarks make an appearance this year, the first such die varieties since 1911. Both are listed in all major references and command high premium values. Repunched mintmarks are also quite prevalent this year, as are doubled dies.

Repunched mintmarks, for the better part, are rather nice and fairly easy to find. Over two dozen RPMs are known for this date. In a recent search through a dozen circulated rolls of 1944-D cents, I found at least one RPM per roll without fail. 1944-S rolls yielded only slightly lower results. I found one example of 1944-D-1OM-002 in circulated rolls and have yet to find an example of the more prominent OMM for the date.

Something else about 1944 mintmarks worth mentioning is that there are two different 'S' mintmark punch styles used this year. The "serif style" used in 1943 makes an appearance this year, as does a new mintmark style, the "ball serif." While both are obtainable, the ball serif style is much more difficult to find. A count of over 500 cents revealed the approximate ratio of ball serif to serif style mintmarks to be approximately 3 to 17.

Doubled dies still show up in the form of class 6 reverses; however, these are less prevalent than in previous years. One thing that does show up quite a bit more this year is class 6 obverses, some of which are extreme in spread. Doubled eyes, while neither as extreme as on 1942 cents nor as numerous as on 1943 cents, are still somewhat prevalent.

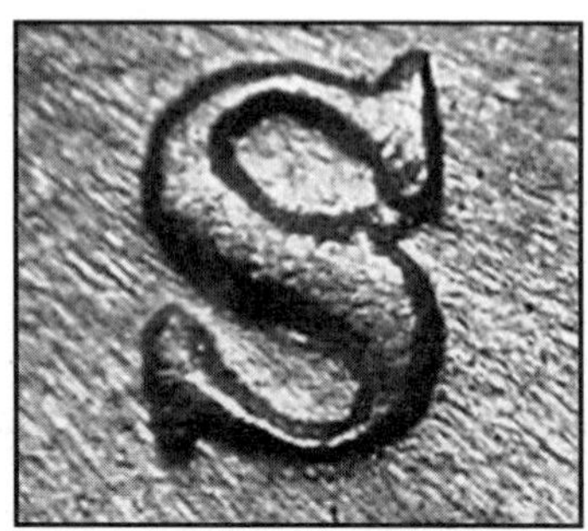

Above: *serif style*

Below: *ball serif style*

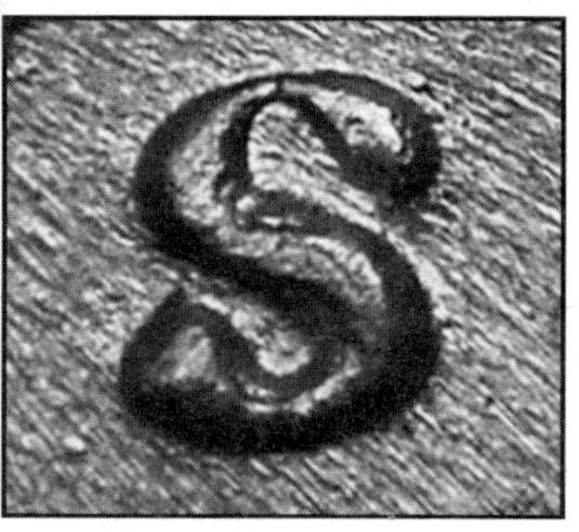

Master die doubling commonly found on 1944 cents appears as doubled corners and serifs on the last two digits of the date. Photo by author.

Watch for another case of master die doubling this year. It occurs on the last two digits of the date and shows as splits in the serifs and light doubling on the outer edges of the devices. This doubling can take on slightly different forms depending on the age of the master die and working hubs at the time the working hubs and working dies were created. They will, however, always have the same split corners of the lower most area of the four digits in the date.

Machine doubling is also quite common this year, as are other minor problems such as lamination and other planchet defects due to impurities in the shellcase bronze used to mint the coins. In fact, this problem seems to carry over to all of the other shellcase bronze cent years (through 1947).

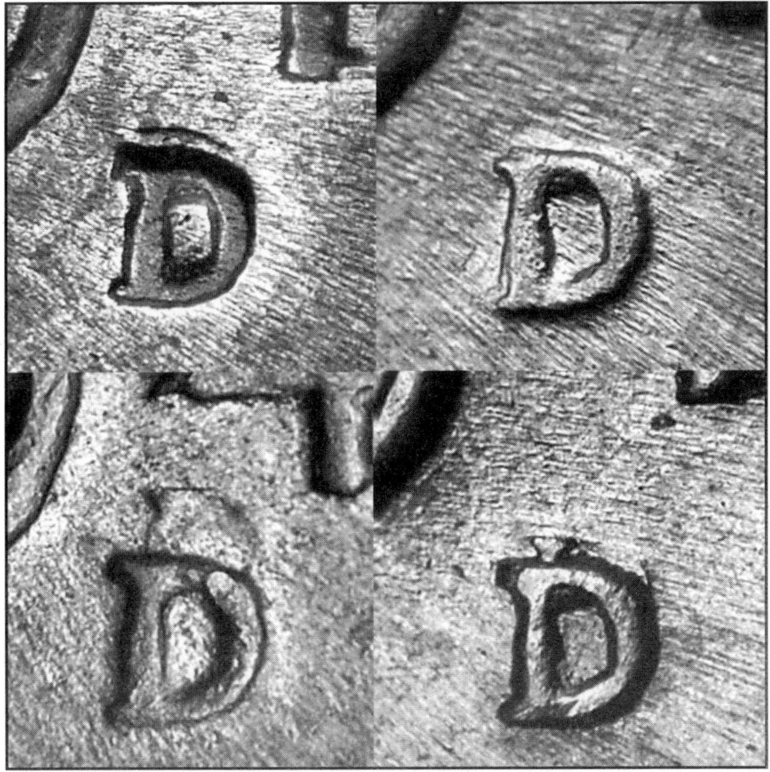

Some of the more common Denver mint RPMs for 1944 are, from top left to bottom right, 1944D-1MM-001, 1944D-1MM-003, 1944D-1MM-007, and 1944D-1MM-008. Many nice repunched mintmarks exist for this date and most are rather easily obtainable. Photos by author.

Above: *1944D-1OM-001 shows the top two thirds of a very well defined S punch centered north of the primary D mintmark. This is the die that commands the highest premium value for the year.*

Below: *1944D-1OM-002 shows a somewhat less obvious S punching centered just to the south of the center of the primary D punching. This die commands about half the premium of its neighbor above.*

1944D-1DO-001 shows very nice extreme class 6 doubling all over the obverse. Take note of the sharp concave points on the left side of the letters in LIBERTY, especially the IB. This is a common trait among class 6 doubled dies that shows on this extreme example better than most others, however it is usually present to some degree on all examples. Photos by author.

1945

Mintage of cents dropped somewhat this year from 1944 levels; however, the number struck is still much higher than any other previous year. For the second year in a row the Philadelphia Mint struck over 1 billion coins — a mark that would not be exceeded again for another 11 years. Quality of strike for this year's issues is usually good, however streaking and discoloration tend to be an issue.

Doubled dies are rather typical for the era, mainly class 6 obverses and reverses. A few class 4 doubled eyelids have also been reported. All told, approximately a dozen different doubled dies are known for the year.

Repunched mintmarks saw a dramatic increase this year — over 40 different dies are currently known, some of which are quite nice. The San Francisco minted RPMs for the year are very difficult to attribute, partly because of the number of dies reported, and partly because many of them are similar in spread and are minor.

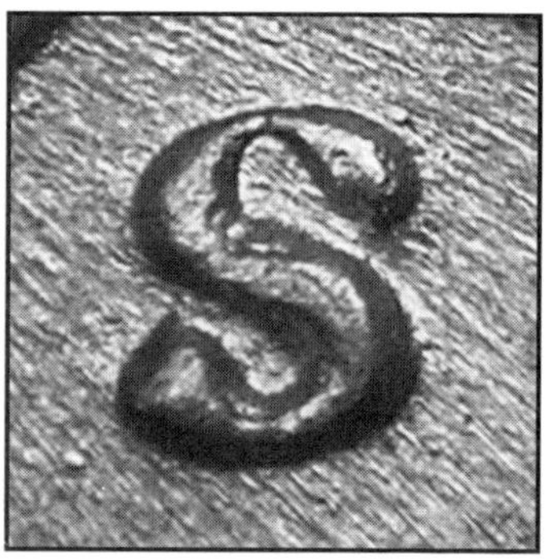

Above: ball serif style

Below: new serif style

This year marks the second year in a row that different styles of mintmark punches were used for the San Francisco Mint dies. Cents can be found with the ball serif style mintmark used in 1944 and with a new serif style mintmark. Although the serif style mintmark is much less common than the ball serif style, very little if any collector value is recognized for this new style of mintmark. If a collector wanted to start saving the potentially more valuable mintmark style before mainstream guides listed it, he or she would want

to go with the new serif style mintmarked coins.

Machine doubling and typical errors that are common for shellcase bronze cents remain a problem this year. 1945 also has a number of CUD die errors, and with some luck and heavy searching, both the pre-CUD retained die breaks and the broken die CUDs can be found to make an interesting pair.

1945S-1DO-001 is a very nice example of a class 6 doubled die obverse. These are rather widespread in 1944 and 1945. Photos by author.

1946

While still quite high, mintage levels dropped again for a second consecutive year. The Philadelphia Mint coined just under a billion cents, Denver was second with just a third that amount, and San Francisco made 198 million cents. Quality is still an issue for the San Francisco minted cents. While those minted in Philadelphia and Denver tend to be a little better, none are as good as 1945. Late die state specimens abound from all mints. However, nice GEM quality earlier die state coins are still available with a little effort.

The class 6 "doubled die machine" that turned out so many dies over the past decade is finally starting to lose steam. Although a few of these 'extra thickness' cents leave the Mint, the number of known class 6 dies from the 1940's is fewer than a half dozen for any given year. There are, however, a number of nice doubled dies this year for which one should watch.

Unbelievably, the number of known RPMs actually increases again over last year's incredible levels. More than 70 different repunched mintmarks are known for this date, nearly doubling the total number of repunched mintmarks known for all dates preceding 1946. For this reason, attributing individual dies must be accomplished with a lot of care, paying attention not only to the exact spread of the RPM, but the markers and exact position of the mintmark as well. In some cases, having a keen eye and a healthy understanding of all these concepts is absolutely necessary to proper die identification.

In the midst of all these repunched mintmarks, be especially observant and you might find one of the rare gems of the Lincoln cent series, 1946S-1OM-001, the only known Lincoln cent over mintmark bearing an 'S' as the primary mintmark. These are very difficult to find in any grade, and are especially rare in higher uncirculated grades.

1946 is yet another year with more than one style of San Francisco mintmark. In fact, this year has three different styles. The two styles used in 1945 are still present (ball serif and serif), and a new sans-serif style emerges.

Since this year was still in the shellcase bronze era, it is easier to find errors than in other years. Laminations tend to be somewhat common, as are streaking and blotchy color on the coins. Since many coins were minted with late die state dies, cracks, breaks, and CUDs are somewhat commonplace, especially on branch mint coins.

In addition to the errors that can show on the coins because of die wear, the wear itself takes on a shape that is often reported as an error. In a number of cases, abraded die doubling (from die wear) caused a shadow effect on the 6 of the date. These are common, as is the other abraded die doubling commonly displayed this year, which features a 6 digit that is weaker looking than the other three digits. None of these effects of die abrasion warrant premium value, as die erosion is a common natural effect of die overuse.

Top: *ball serif style*
Center: *serif style*
Bottom: *sans-serif style*

1946S-1OM-001 is the only known example in the Lincoln cent series of an S mintmark over a D mintmark. The D starts at the base of the S and goes upward to within the upper loop of the S. These are very rare in uncirculated grades and quite scarce in all other grades. Photo by author.

1946S-1DO-003 shows nice class 2 distorted hub doubling in the first two digits of the date. Photo by author.

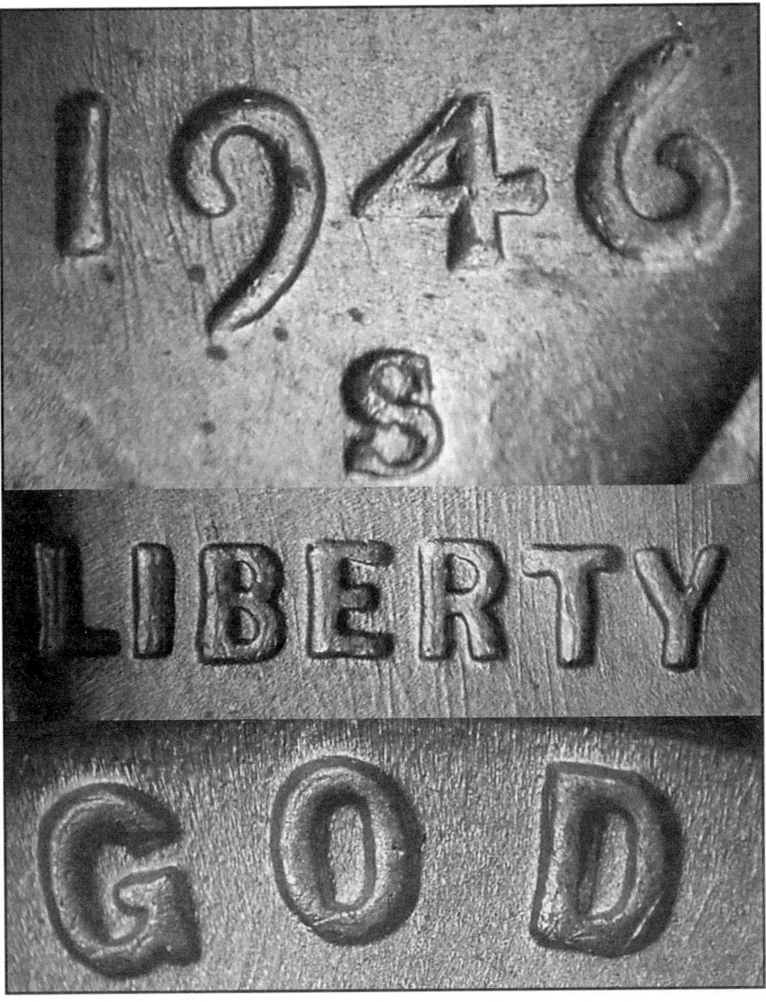

1946S-1DO-005 shows very nice doubling in LIBERTY and to the of the date. Minor doubling shows in the GO of GOD. This is a nice example of class 2 distorted hub doubling. Photos by author.

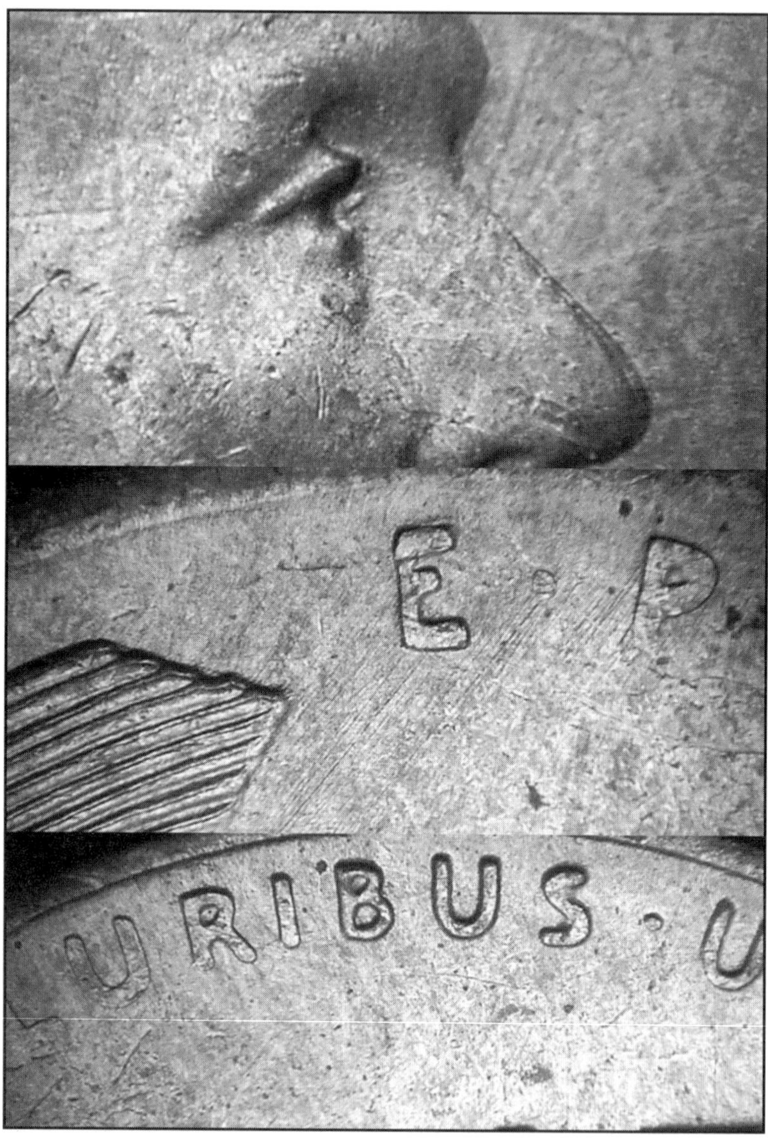

Although minor, 1946S-1DO-002, 1946S-1DR-001 shows the importance of always looking on the other side of the coin when you find a die variety. These doubled dies are on the same coin. Photos by author.

1947

The last year of shellcase bronze cents comes with a reduction in mintage. The post-war economy is in recession and the overproduction of cents during the last three years has filled the shortage created by the ill-fated steel cents and the war. As an effect, production drops significantly this year. For the second time in the Lincoln cent history, the Denver Mint made more cents than the main mint in Philadelphia. The San Francisco Mint made fewer than 100 million cents this year, compared to an average of 200 million minted through the latter half of World War II.

These lower mintage numbers did not significantly affect the 1947cent. Bags and rolls were hoarded, thus uncirculated coins from all three mints are still available by the roll. Prices for the uncirculated specimens remain virtually the same as those made over the past three years. Circulated coins are common throughout this period.

Production decreases did little to affect the quality of coins minted. The branch mint cents still suffer from having been minted with overused dies, as is evident in the number of coins found with die cracks, die breaks, and overall die erosion. Philadelphia minted cents are the best in strike quality, however many cents minted this year suffer from planchet striping, blotchiness, and discoloration. Finding true GEM uncirculated cents takes a good deal of searching.

Doubled dies are down again this year from last year's paltry levels. Class 6 and class 2 doubled die reverses number fewer than a half dozen known dies, and class 4 eyelids comprise most of the half dozen or so known obverses. No doubled dies have been reported to date on Denver minted 1947 cents. A couple of nice doubled dies are known, and those typically bring healthy premiums in higher grades.

Repunched mintmarks are way down in the number known as well. There are just over a dozen known dies between the two branch mints, down from last year by 80 percent. Because of this decline and the overall lack of quality in 1947 branch mint cents, nice GEM examples of repunched mintmarks are worth nearly 25 percent more on average. None of the known 1947 repunched mintmarks are much more than split serifs and minor curve splits.

The sans-serif and serif styles of mintmark punches from 1946 carry over to this year. The sans-serif is slightly less common, but not enough to affect value. Both styles are relatively easy to find while viewing a rather small sampling of coins.

 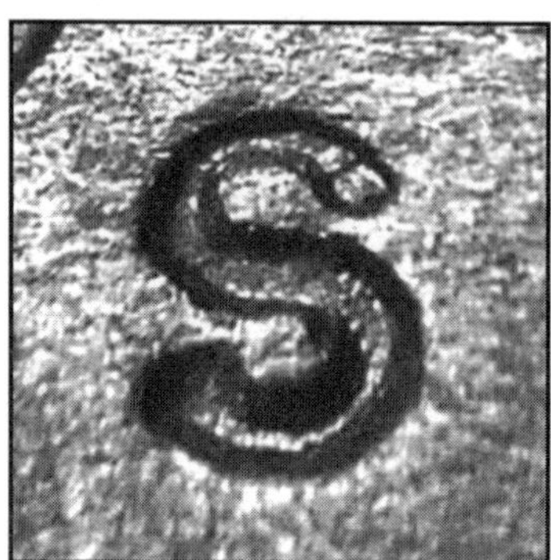

Left: *serif style.* **Right**: *sans-serif style*

Two of the nicer RPMs for 1947 — these are 1947D-1MM-001 and 1947S-1MM-002. None of the RPMs for 1947 are easy to find. These are among the more common dies one will likely encounter. Photos by author.

1947P-1DO-001 shows nice pivoted hub doubling (class 5) all over the obverse, especially in the date. These are very scarce in uncirculated grades. Photos by author, coin by Brian Maguire.

1948

Production was up again as the post-war economy began to bounce back from recession. Nearly twice the number of cents were minted compared to 1947, yet the quality did not improve much. Soft details continue to be the general rule, although higher grade, sharply struck coins are available.

Doubled dies continue to be on the down side as most examples found are minor. Class 6 obverses are the most typical, but be wary that master die doubling in the form of a minor class 6 spread shows on many coins minted this year. Like with all other examples of master die doubling, little or no premium value is warranted because it is extremely common.

Repunched mintmarks are up by a few from last year, but are still far short of levels produced in 1946. Around a dozen different repunched mintmarks are known for each branch mint. None of the known repunched mintmarks are major or particularly valuable for this year.

Some unsubstantiated reports have surfaced that there is more than one style of mintmark found on 1948-S cents. The reports indicate that the sans-serif style mintmark introduced in 1946 was still used on some 1948-S cents. I have not seen any examples of mintmarks other than the now standard serif style mintmark introduced in 1945. Please report any coins you find to the contrary.

Overall, a noticeably dull year is in store while searching through 1948 cents.

Master die doubling visible on most 1948 cents shows as light extra thickness especially noticeable in TRUST. Photo by author.

Three of the repunched mintmarks for 1948-D. These are, from left to right, 1948D-1MM-004, 1948D-1MM-005, and 1948D-1MM-008.

1948S-1DO-002 shows abundant extra thickness in Lincoln's face and in the motto. All of the details on this coin are very soft, to include the last digit in the date. This die erosion is common for 1948 cents. Photos by author.

1949

Cent production is up overall this year, but the San Francisco Mint's production is down by over 15 million coins. What would otherwise be a rather quiet year is stirred by this shortage. 1949-S cents in high grade are sought after by collectors and carry a little more value than other coins of this period — which is ironic considering the 1949-S cents are slightly more plentiful.

There are few known doubled dies of mention this year, but repunched mintmarks continue at around a dozen known per mint. A few of the repunched mintmarks are nice, but many are rather minor and worth a bit less than other die varieties of the era.

A new '4' digit was put into place this year in the date. It has a squared-off top as opposed to the pointed top used on 1948 cents. One of the two reported doubled dies for 1949-S involves what is apparently a squared-off '4' over a pointed '4'. While no examples have been found of a pointed top 1949 cent, one should watch for this possibility when searching through coins.

1949D-1MM-001 shows a tripled mintmark as a nice spread to the northeast and doubled serifs. Photo by author.

1949S-1DO-001 shows what is apparently a squared-off 4 hubbed over a pointed 4. Doubling also shows to the southeast in the date and to the southwest in LIBERTY. This is a class 3 design hub doubled coin — two different designs hubbed into the same die. This die also indicates there is a chance that there are other 1949 pointed-top cents out there, but this author has never seen one. Photos by Bob Piazza.

1950

1950 marked the first year since the beginning of World War II that proof sets were issued from the Philadelphia Mint. At the same time, production of Lincoln cents also dropped at the Philadelphia Mint. While the issuance of proof sets may not be the exact cause of the drop in cent production for circulation, the fact remains that Philadelphia produced only 81 percent of the output of the Denver Mint.

Even with lower production, the cents from Philadelphia continue on a quality down swing. Late die state specimens are common, and coins often suffer discoloration from chemical washes at the Mint. Denver Mint cents show signs of the same quality woes. San Francisco cents, however, are often found in full red GEM condition.

Doubled dies are at a near complete stand still this year. Only a few are known, the only one of real note is on an obverse die from Denver. Doubled eyelid cents are quite possible; one die is known from the Philadelphia Mint.

Repunched mintmarks, however, are still going strong in 1950. Nearly a dozen different dies are known for the Denver Mint, and nearly two dozen for the San Francisco Mint, with new discoveries in minor split serif RPMs made regularly.

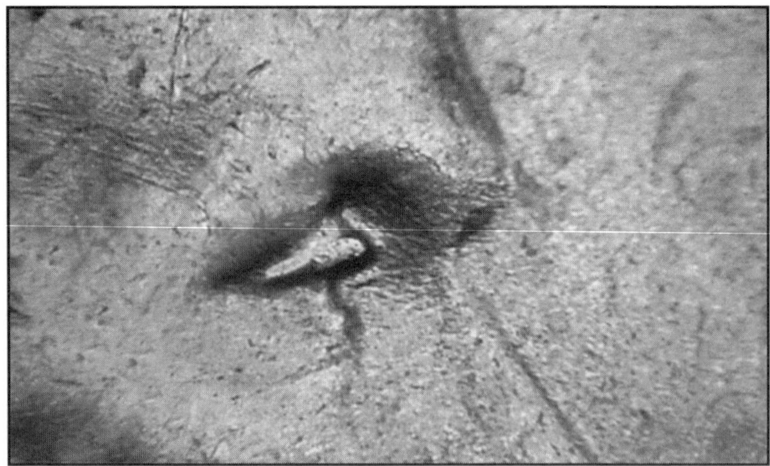

1950P-1DO-001 is the one known doubled eyelid for the date. Photo by author.

1950D-1DO-001 is the sole known doubled die obverse for 1950-D cents. Notice the doubling as a minor south spread in LIBERTY. The date and mintmark are shown for mintmark placement verification. Photos by author.

1951

1951 presents us with yet another year in which the Denver Mint produced far more cents than the Philadelphia Mint. One explanation for the lower numbers from the main facility is that Philadelphia had just begun minting proof coins in 1950, and was still adjusting to the new production demands during this year.

Improved technology at the Philadelphia Mint gave them the ability to produce more coins at a lower cost. As a trade off, however, quality seems to have suffered. Finding true GEM red specimens of 1951 plain cents is rather difficult, though possible. Issues from Denver and San Francisco tend to be of only slightly better quality than the Philadelphia minted coins. Incomplete, soft strikes are common, and show as softness and incomplete outlines around the O of ONE on the reverse. Later die state coins are also common.

Doubled dies aren't any more available this year than last; fewer than half a dozen are known for the date. One of these doubled dies looks almost like a carbon copy of a die from 1950 with a light spread on the bottom of the letters in LIBERTY. Doubled eyelids exist this year as well, so don't forget to check for them.

Mintmark varieties take a huge turn upward this year. Enough nice repunched mintmarks are known to make this year's branch mint coins a favorite for many roll searchers. Two different over mintmarks are known for D mint cents, and over four dozen RPMs are known for the date; three fourths of them are from the Denver Mint.

Another anomaly makes an appearance this year. While visible at times on previous years' cents, reduction lathe doubling on the front of the profile of Lincoln's bust becomes more commonplace this year. These have been reported as doubled dies a number of times, which they are not. They are the result of maladjustment on the lathe used to reduce the design from the large plaster model of the design, and are not a result of the hubbing process itself.

Machine doubling is also rather common this year, as are die chips and die breaks. It seems that the Mint was trying to get more life out of each die, as many very late die state coins have been observed that were minted with dies that are nearly falling apart.

Above: *1951P-1DO-002 shows light doubling on the bottom of the letters in LIBERTY.*

Below: *1951P-1DO-003 shows light doubling on the bottom of the L and B of LIBERTY and to the left of the I of IN. Photos by aurthor.*

This example of 1951P-1DO-001P submitted by Steve Eckhouse shows very nice distorted hub doubling (class 2) toward the center of the coin on the motto and date. While doubled dies are much less common on proof coins, they are easier to spot because of the relative sharpness of detail. Photos by author.

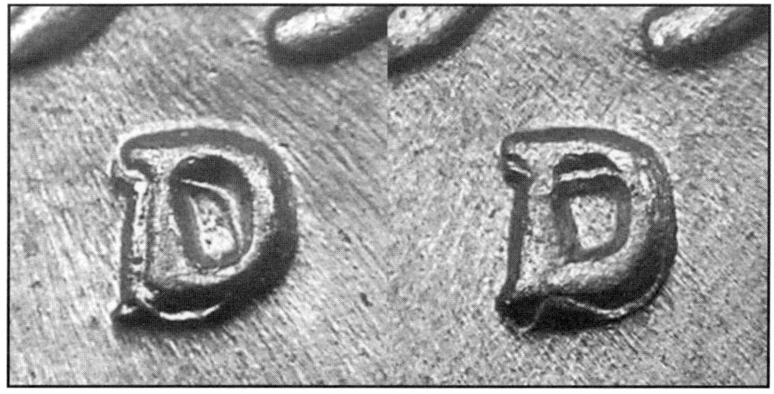

Top Left: *1951D-1MM-001 is one of the nicest RPMs for the date.*

Top Right: *1951D-1MM-004 shows a very distinct spread to the south.*

Bottom Left: *1951D-1MM-010 shows a strong spread to the east.*

Bottom Right: *1951D-1MM-016 shows a moderately hubbed strong spread to the south. This RPM is often mistaken for 1951D-1OM-002. The main readily visible difference between them is the sharp line inside this RPM which is absent in the OMM. Photos by author.*

1951D-1OM-001 (above) and 1951D-1OM-002 (below) show parts of S mintmarks punched along with the D mintmarks. 1951D-1OM-001 is among the most difficult of Lincoln cent OMMs to locate because it is so difficult to detect. Photos by author.

1952

Philadelphia and San Francisco minted cents this year tend to be well struck but are usually discolored and spotted. Superlative GEM (MS-67) examples are nearly unheard of in all but Denver minted cents. This, coupled with a relatively low mintage in plain and S mint cents and a lack of availability of original rolls, has pushed roll prices to near $100. Meanwhile, Denver Mint roll prices remain comparable to surrounding years at around $10 per roll. Finding uncirculated rolls of plain and S mint cents from this year is rather difficult at best.

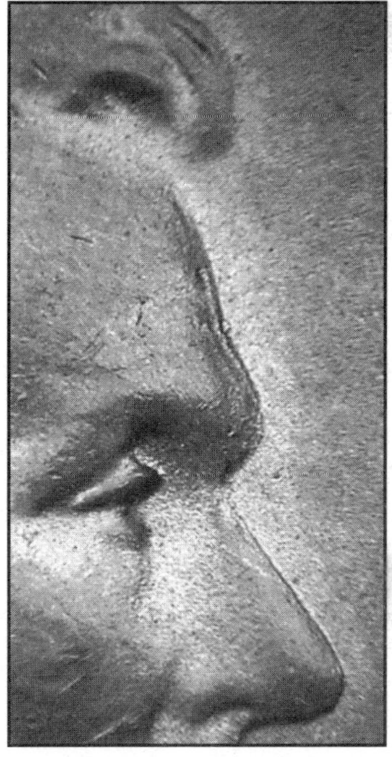

Reduction lathe doubling seen on the forehead in this photo is common for 1952 cents. It is not a doubled die.

Doubled dies are very minimal and quite minor this year. Most of the half dozen known doubled dies are doubled eyelids, and the other doubled dies for the year are not readily visible and do not command much premium.

Master die doubling shows on many 1952 cents in the form of doubling in the date. These, as with all other cases of master die doubling, do not carry any premium value.

Another anomaly that is commonly reported as a doubled die shows on this years' cents as well. Described in the 1951 section (see above), reduction lathe doubling is very common on 1952 cents. Most early to middle die state examples examined exhibit this common form of doubling and, thus, do not command any premium value.

Mintmark varieties for this year, on the other hand, are the most numerous for any date in wheat reverse cents. At the time of this printing, over 100 different dies have been discovered with new discoveries added regularly. A problem exists, however, with the D

A broken punch is to blame for the split lower serif on this mintmark. It is not an RPM.

mintmark punch. Many examples sent in as RPMs show a damaged lower serif in the punch and are not RPMs. These are among the most common non-RPM coins sent in as such.

One very odd RPM for the date shows a partial D punched beneath Lincoln's lapel at the rim. This RPM is easy to miss and is quite valuable. So far very few uncirculated specimens have been reported, while circulated specimens seem to be uncommon to scarce, but not rare.

An over mintmark also exists this year. A nicely defined S punch is visible, spread to the south of the primary D mintmark. While this OMM is rather scarce, it is known in very late die state, so it is suspected that a large number of coins exhibiting this OMM exist. This is the least valuable of all known Lincoln cent OMMs, averaging $25 for uncirculated specimens.

Die breaks in the date and mintmark area tend to be very common in 1952 because the dies used this year, especially those in Philadelphia, saw far more use than they should have. Some of these die breaks are major enough to warrant a premium value ranging between $1 and $5. Do not expect to see a price guide listing for these, as collector interest is very specific and small.

Elaborate die breaks such as the one seen here are rather common for 1952 cents. Some of them are worth a modest premium value as a curiosity. Photo by author.

Master die doubling shows in different areas of the date (arrows) on many 1952 cents. Photo by author.

1952D-1MM-025 actually has four mintmarks — can you spot them all? Look inside the primary mintmark and beneath the primary mintmark for hints. It can be difficult to spot some of the less obvious RPMs!

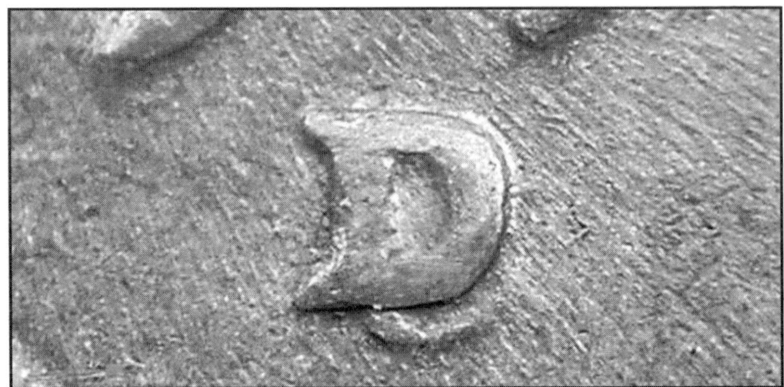

1952D-1OM-001 shows an extra S curve to the south of the D mintmark. This OMM is the most common, thus least valuable of all Lincoln cent OMMs. Photo by author.

1952P-1DO-001 is very commonly missed because not many people know about it. It shows nice doubling in TRUST. Photos by Bob Piazza.

1953

Mintage was a little higher than 1952 for all three mints combined, but not by much. The gain Philadelphia and San Francisco made was set off by lower mintage by the Denver Mint. The increase in mintage, however, was not enough to answer for the much lower roll prices experienced by this year's cents. GEM uncirculated coins are readily available. However, they will take a modest amount of searching to find. Late die state coins from overused dies are still a problem, especially in Philadelphia and San Francisco minted coins. Because of this, die breaks, die cracks, and other problems associated with extended die life are all problems commonly exhibited this year.

The 1953 proof cent is first in a couple of things. It was the first proof issue of the Lincoln cent series that saw a mintage of more than 100,000. It is also the first issue on which a nice doubled die obverse is known. Very rare and difficult to obtain, this doubled die shows mostly in the date with a very nice spread to the southeast on the 19 and extra thickness on all digits.

Overall, doubled dies are very scattered this year. With fewer than half a dozen known dies, there is nothing regular between them, and most are rather minor. The aforementioned proof doubled die obverse is definitely the centerpiece of 1953 doubled dies.

Repunched mintmarks are very numerous this year with over 70 different known dies. However, many of these are rather minor and take skill and care to attribute. With this many different dies, there are still some real nice ones for which one should watch. One Denver minted example has the widest spreads of all Lincoln cent RPMs and is quite exciting to find.

Abraded die doubling, especially on the last digit of the date, becomes a problem this year. Although visible on some coins from some earlier years, entire rolls of this "shadow doubling" are not difficult to spot this year. These are caused by extreme die wear and age, and are not true hub doubled dies. Being that they are easy to find and are not doubled dies, they should command little if any premium value, and primarily serve as a conversation piece.

Abraded die doubling such as that seen here is common for the later die state cents struck this year. These are often mistaken for doubled dies. Photo by author.

1953P-1DO-001P shows nice doubling on the first three digits of the date. This doubled die is odd in that it is the earliest known example of a proof doubled die with a spread as nice as this one. In later years doubled dies with such spreads will become somewhat more common. Photo by author.

This year is known for nice repunched mintmarks. Above, 1953D-1MM-002 shows one of the nicest spreads to the west of any Lincoln cent RPM. Below, 1953S-1MM-002 shows a very well defined spread to the east. Notice how the mintmark is touching the 5 of the date. Since mintmarks were applied by hand, awkward positioning of the mintmark is actually rather common. Photos by author.

1954

Mintage fell dramatically this year partly because of a fall in demand for new coins. The Philadelphia Mint coined the lowest number of cents since 1933, and production at the branch mints fell by an average of 50 percent. GEM uncirculated coins are somewhat difficult to find from San Francisco, and are very scarce from Philadelphia. In fact, Philadelphia minted 1954 cents sell for well over $10 in true MS-65 or better, and certified high grade examples sell for far more — easily into the hundreds of dollars. Because rolls are readily available (although usually low in quality) they sell for around $10 each from any of the three mints.

Doubled dies are quite scattered this year as well. One issue from San Francisco shows a nice distorted spread in the date and motto. This very late die state is possibly one of the nicest and most common double dies in the series. Doubled eyelids are not out of the question this year, though only one is known.

Repunched mintmarks, while not as numerous as the past two years, are still widespread. A dozen Denver Mint and over two dozen San Francisco Mint issues are

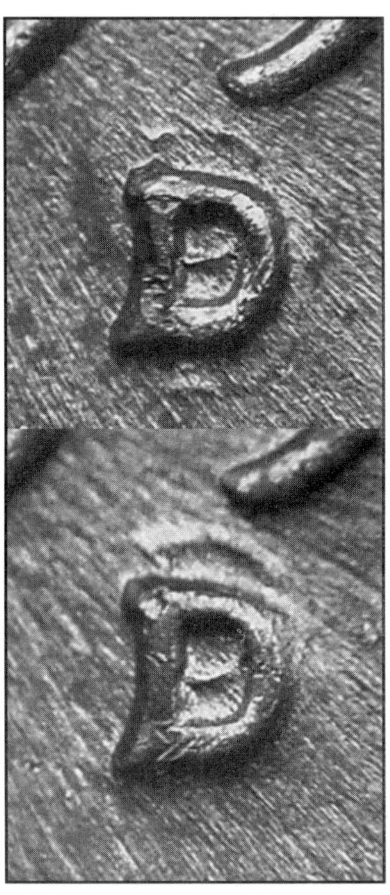

1954D-1MM-001 is a good example of how die wear can erode the attributes of a nice RPM making later die state examples less valuable. The top image shows all three punchings because it is MDS, and the photo on the bottom is the same die in LDS with the south repunching worn away. Photos by author.

known. Because many of the RPMs for this year are known in very late die state, they are also considered common. Thus, they do not warrant much premium value. Many of the nicer yet more common repunched mintmarks for this date are shown following the text.

One repunched mintmark for D mint cents is the first in a special case of die varieties that have differing value depending on the die state of the coin. 1954D-1MM-001 shows a very nice north and south tripled mintmark spread in earlier die states. However, as the die wore the south spread disappeared. Because of this, the later die state coins are less dramatic and thus less valuable than their earlier die state counterparts. There are a number of cases in the die varieties of the series that do have different values because the wear on the die hides some of the detail the die once had, thus detrimentally affecting its interest factor.

Abraded die doubling such as that seen here is very common on 1954 cents. Do not confuse these for valuable doubled dies. Photo by author.

A die break fills the 9 of the date on a 1954 cent. These are quite common throughout the 1950's.

Abraded die doubling is a problem yet again this year. A number of late die state and very late die state coins have been observed with doubling from abrasion in LIBERTY, the motto, and the date (especially in the last digit). See and read more about abraded die doubling in the 1955 text.

As with the past couple of years, die breaks and cracks are also common on 1954 cents. Except for major examples, do not expect these to command much, if any, premium value.

Above and Below: *1954S-1MM-001, 002, 003, and 004 show the diversity of nice repunched mintmarks for 1954-S cents. Notice that 1954S-1MM-001* **(top left)** *has quite a bit of die wear. This is indicative that this variety is rather common. 1954S-1MM-003* **(below left)** *shows a very interesting wide spread to the northwest. While 1954S-1MM-004* **(below right)** *has a very nice looking north spread, it is also known in VLDS and thus is considered rather common. Photos by author.*

1954S-1DO-001 shows a nice class 2 distorted spread, but is one of the most common doubled dies with a nice spread in the Lincoln cent series. Notice the die cracks on the date. Photos by author.

1955

Because of a lack of modernization and budgetary constraints, the U.S. Mint decided to shut down its facility in San Francisco this year. The last Lincoln cents to bear the S mintmark (so they thought) were minted on March 24th , and the facility went back to being an assay office as it had started back in 1851.

When the news of the facility's demise reached the public, it sparked an unprecedented mass hoarding of the cents made in San Francisco. Thousands of mint-fresh bags were saved, as were a large number of original uncirculated rolls. Ironically, these rolls still command a premium over those issued in similar quantities for other years. Because they have been a centerpiece of attention for wheat cents as the final S mint issue, the San Francisco minted cents are very common in most grades and can be found in GEM and superlative GEM grades at reasonable prices.

Quality of 1955 cents is all around questionable at best. Philadelphia minted cents are quite often marred by spots, die cracks, and very soft details. Die wear problems at the Philadelphia Mint prove to be the most extreme since the 1920's. Denver and San Francisco issues are not much better, though somewhat sharper details should be expected on these issues. GEM mint state examples from Philadelphia command a nice premium, especially when certified MS-66 or higher.

1955P-1DO-001 is arguably the doubled die that started the die variety collecting market. Photo courtesy of the Stewart Blay collection.

Perhaps considered one of the most famous years of the Lincoln cent by many generalist numismatists and collectors, 1955 is actually somewhat lacking in many areas. Save a very strong doubled die obverse that arguably started the die variety craze, only a few doubled dies show up

Master die damage shows on a 1955-D cent. Photo by author.

this year. Repunched mintmarks are quite low in number as well, averaging a dozen different known dies per branch mint.

Master die damage caused doubling in the upper BE of LIBERTY on many cents this year. It is very common on cents from all three mints and should not be mistaken for a doubled die.

To avoid republishing the same information ad-nauseum regarding the highly sought after 1955 doubled die obverse specimen, I strongly encourage readers to either study long and hard before purchasing a raw specimen or to only buy 1955 doubled dies in holders certified by a reputable grading service. Counterfeits are widespread and very easily fool those who do not know the variety well. See the special article following the text for this year to learn about some of the deceptive doubled die counterfeits for this die.

As a result of this issue's widespread following, original bank wrapped rolls of 1955 plain cents have sold for exponential factors above published roll values. I have seen reportedly unopened rolls sell to speculators for $150 to $175 on more than one occasion. Extreme caution should be exercised when buying rolls of this date for a premium because they are reportedly bank-fresh unopened rolls. Coin rolls are relatively easy to unwrap, look through, and re-wrap. Good judgment in this case is the key.

1955-P cents with abraded die doubling (from die erosion) are typically called "Poor Man's Double Dies" even though they have nothing to do with hub doubling. They are very common, but because of their traditional following, they often sell for a premium. Photo by author.

Because 1955 plain cents are usually of very poor quality and because of the very famous doubled die issue, an anomaly commonly found on many dates of Lincoln cents where die quality is in question becomes the subject of mistaken identity this year. Abraded die doubling, caused by the chipping outward of extremely worn dies, gives the appearance that the outer devices on the coin are doubled. In this case, of special note is the last 5 in the date, which by its shape and the nature of extremely worn dies used this year, can be impressive looking. This abraded die doubling on 1955 cents is commonly referred to as the "poor man's double die."

The exact origin of the poor man's double die (which is not a doubled die at all) is unknown, but it is known that they began surfacing shortly after the news of the doubled die hit the mainstream press. Thousands upon thousands of onlookers who had never looked at the date on a "penny" before were finding these abraded die doubled cents and taking them in to coin dealers for their fast cash, only to be disappointed when finding out that these were only normal cents.

Over the years that followed the value of the 1955 doubled die cent skyrocketed, sending it well beyond the reach of most collectors. Possibly because of the same misunderstanding that took the public by surprise, but more likely the advertising genius of the dealers who had these coins, these abraded doubled cents were offered in magazines as a poor man's version of the real doubled die. The term sticks to this date, and even though many people know the reason for this doubling is actually quite common, the story behind these coins keeps their premium value around $5, which is far more than they are worth.

A sign of the times for 1955 cents, this coin was struck with extremely worn and obstructed (dirty) dies. Photos by author.

One of the more difficult RPMs to locate in modern wheat cents is this 1955S-1MM-001. Only known in early and mid-die state, it is evident that there were not very many of these made. This die typically sells for close to $20 in GEM uncirculated grades. Photo by author.

Even the proof cents have quite a bit to offer, with nearly half a dozen different doubled die reverses known. This is 1955P-1DR-001P. Photos by author.

Two of the nicer RPMs for 1955-D, these are 1955D-1MM-002 (left) and 1955D-1MM-004 (right). They are similar in spread so attribute them carefully. Photos by author.

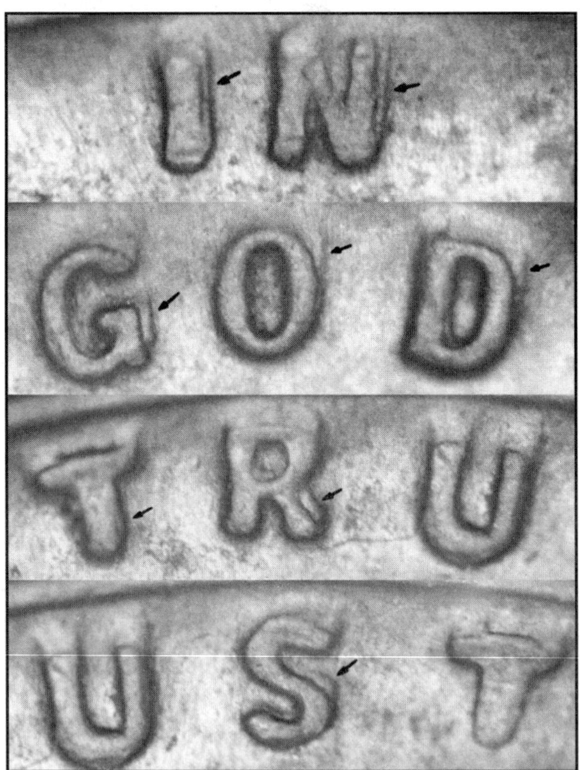

1955P-1DO-002 is a quite rare and valuable doubled die that many skip because the doubling, although very well spread, is quite weakly hubbed. If it had not been for the fame of 1955P-1DO-001, this doubled die would have been the crown gem of the year. Photos courtesy of Billy Crawford.

1955D-1DO-001 provides us with an interesting doubled eye — one of the strongest known in the Lincoln cent series. Notice also that the first two digits of the date are doubled as well. Photos by Bob Piazza.

1955 Struck Counterfeit Doubled Die Case Study

> This article was originally published in March, 2003 on the author's website, www.coppercoins.com. It is being republished here in its entirety because the author believes it is very important to disseminate such information as widely as possible.

It is always wise to be very wary of what you purchase, especially when it comes to buying valuable coins. The purpose of this page is to help you determine whether that "king of kings" doubled die you have your eye on is genuine.

The specifics of this document and the photographs that follow are an example of what to watch for in struck counterfeits of valuable coins — this by no means is the only type of counterfeit nor is it the only die with which struck counterfeits are made, so do not pick any specific markers off of the photos of the counterfeit below and read them as being exactly what to look for in determining a 1955 doubled die to be counterfeit or genuine. Since there are other methods and other counterfeit dies used, certification or authentication BEFORE purchase is the only sure way to tell whether you have the "real deal" or a fake. Reading a bit between the lines, you can derive from my statement that you should either know VERY WELL what you are doing in buying an uncertified specimen, or stick to certified (slabbed) specimens.

The struck counterfeit documented here was sent in by K. Reichert, who was genuinely gracious in allowing me to examine this piece after having received it back from ANACS as a struck counterfeit. Very luckily, he is going to be refunded for this coin, but his case is an exception. MANY people are fooled by these coins because the method used to create them is very close to that which made the genuine specimens. Without detailed analysis it is very difficult to tell the difference between them.

This macro image (facing page) of the struck counterfeit looks quite convincing. In fact, without magnification it is very difficult even for a seasoned specialist to detect. The only real sign of a counterfeit from this viewpoint is the rim of the coin. If compared to just about any other

Struck
Counterfeit

genuine cent from that era, it is a curiosity that the rim is nearly razor sharp and the edges of the coin are more rounded-off than a genuine cent. Other than that, this coin (without magnification) could easily be passed off as genuine. Its weight is within tolerance of a genuine cent (3.10 grams), its thickness is about right, and it appears to be made of the correct alloy.

Since more detail is required to assess the problems with the counterfeit, I have taken the liberty of using photographs of a genuine 1955 doubled die to compare with this struck counterfeit. The genuine doubled die, at the time it was photographed, belonged to collector Jim Hiironen. I use the genuine coin to compare to the counterfeit more so that you can see the differences side by side, but viewing a genuine coin at the same time as a counterfeit is not entirely necessary nor is it often possible. In that, it is important that you be able to recognize the characteristics of the counterfeit as it stands alone, not just in a side by side comparison with a known genuine specimen.

The first photograph shows immediate problems that will carry forward to other photographs below. Note the thickness difference in the rim as described above. Also notice the acute flatness of the devices on the counterfeit. They seem rather wide, yet flat. The overall relief is lower, and the devices are the wrong distance from the rim. Notice how close IN GOD is from the rim on the counterfeit.

Another problem that will be revisited throughout these photographs is that some of the devices (such as the D in this photo) are unusually thicker than other devices on the counterfeit. Notice the equal thickness of different features on the genuine coin.

The next image carries forth all of the previously mentioned problems, but adds another problem to the list. Notice the weakness and flatness to the left side of the W on the counterfeit. It is very likely that the planchet used for this coin was not subjected to an upset mill to raise 

the rim. Rather, the field of the die was curved to assimilate the relief of the rim. When the W was hubbed into the die, it was hubbed too closely to the curved rim and came out incomplete on top. A genuine 1955 doubled die will not show this sort of characteristic anywhere on the coin.

I think it is very important to stress that this particular problem is evident on the W in WE on this particular counterfeit, but is by no

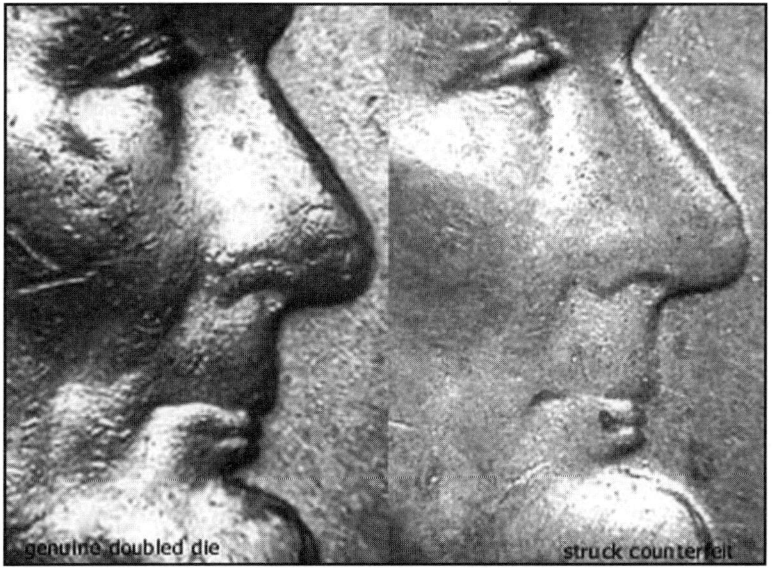

means an absolute with all struck counterfeits. Weakness may show in a different area of a different counterfeit.

The face (actually the entire bust) shows notable weakness in detail, quite visible in this particular example as a lack of lower nose detail — namely the separation line that shows on the genuine specimen is non-existent on the counterfeit. The doubling shows above the eye on the counterfeit, but shows a distinct lack of shape to the primary eyelid, another "sign."

Notice also the general lack of sharpness to the bridge of the nose, nostril, front of the eye, the crease in the lip, and the crease in front of the cheek. The list goes on and is evident throughout the design; this photo should be enough to give a general idea of the overall weakness in the counterfeit. The detail in the hair, ear, coat, and shoulder folds also carry this weakness.

The area around LIBERTY (top of next page) is where these particular counterfeiters went really wrong. Notice how the L crowds the rim in the counterfeit, and it is quite misshapen by this. Again, this won't necessarily be the case with all struck counterfeits, but something like this may be apparent with any number of them.

Notice also the lack of detail, namely separation lines, in the letters. Oddly enough, though, one of the signs of a genuine 1955 doubled die

does show here — the angled "cut" across the top of the E. This is a feature of nearly all 1955 cents and serves as a valuable lesson: don't look for just one feature. Observe all the details.

The last feature to cover on the obverse is the date. Both coins show the weak top of the 1, an apparent sign on all genuine 1955 cents. Once again, study the whole piece. Signs of genuine attributes will often come through on counterfeits.

Notice, however, that there is a distinct "cut" between the 1 digits on the counterfeit. Again, a tooling effect probably done to separate the devices from one another to make the finished product look more genuine.

As mentioned above, the date digits appear to be somewhat shallower in the counterfeit, as well as more squared-off in relief.

Take note also that one of the markers for a genuine 1955 doubled die, the light NW-SE die scratches through the date are not present on the counterfeit.

Finally, the reverse. This particular reverse shows a light class 2 doubled die with minor separation showing in the motto and right wheat lines. Of course, the genuine doubled dies do not show this doubling. The relief on the entire reverse is also too shallow for a genuine coin. Interestingly enough, the top of the O in ONE is complete, which is a common weak point in genuine wheat cents. This can be attributed to the low relief being able to strike up more detail with less pressure.

The other typically known marker (sorry, no photo) is the X shaped die scratch to the left of the T in CENT. The counterfeit does not show this marker, although it does have die scratches in that area that could be mistaken for the die scratches on the genuine doubled die. One of the problems with using these die scratches as the only key for determining a coin to be real is that often the color or luster (or lack of) will effectively hide the presence of these scratches. Weak strike or any number of other slight anomalies can also make them weak and nearly invisible. Also important is the fact that the counterfeit shows a criss-cross pattern of very light and very thin die scratches throughout the reverse, which is not present on genuine specimens.

1956

The first year since 1934 that saw mintage at only two facilities, 1956 also boasts the first single facility mintage above one billion coins in over a decade. In fact, mintage at Philadelphia and Denver this year exceeded the combined mintage of all three facilities in any year since 1946. Although quality is still an issue, especially on the reverse, GEM specimens are readily obtainable and are inexpensive. Original rolls survive in the thousands, although they are drying up fast because of die varieties.

Doubled dies are dominated this year by doubled eyelids. Over a dozen different dies have been separated, and there are likely many more to catalog. Other than the doubled eyelids, there are very few other doubled dies known for this year. The mintmark varieties are the star attraction for 1956.

The mintmark varieties for 1956-D cents, when combined, offer more bang for the buck for cherrypickers than any other year in the Lincoln cent series. Two known OMMs and three known completely separated RPMs head up the crowd, and half a dozen nice examples of more typical RPMs round off the top twenty dies for the date. Trailing behind those are at least a dozen different split serif RPMs that are generally difficult to attribute and do not command much premium or collector interest.

The main oddity behind the OMMs for 1956-D is that the San Francisco Mint shut down in March of 1955 (see the 1955 text above). One theory behind the reason why S mintmarks were applied to 1956 dies is that the dies had been prepared prior to the announcement of the San Francisco Mint shutting down and then were changed to Denver Mint dies after the closure was announced. Although this seems plausible, it is unlikely.

First, dies are not prepared a year ahead of time, and that would have to be the case for 1956 dies to have been prepared before mint officials planned to shut San Francsico down. Second, the location of the S mintmark on one of the OMMs is far outside the normal placement, showing that this had to be a mistake, not a purposefully punched die. Whatever the case, these OMMs exist and are very interesting and valuable.

Overall, 1956-D cents are among the most exciting and rewarding for roll searching throughout the entire series. For this reason, 1956-D bags are likely gone and original rolls are moving as fast as they can be found. Having sold for as little as $3 within the past five years, a collector is lucky today to find original rolls. When they do, they are lucky to get them for anything under $10. Pieced-together rolls of uncirculated 1956-D cents are common and generally still sell for under $10. Circulated rolls are common and a suggested means of locating some of the nice gems that await the patient hunter.

Although 1956D-1MM-001 is a very impressive repunched mintmark, they are quite common. This die is known to have lasted through late die state, which indicates that it minted at least a quarter million coins. Even with that in mind, it still brings over $10 in uncirculated grades because of its impressive spread. Photo by Richard S. Cooper.

By far one of the most unusual RPMs in the Lincoln cent series is 1956D-1MM-008, an RPM with a completely detached extra mintmark to the south. These are described as, "D and D," instead of the typical, "D/D," because of the complete separation of the secondary mintmark from the primary mintmark. These are quite rare and highly sought after. The main pickup point is that the primary mintmark is located so closely to the 56 of the date. Photo by author.

Another one of the highly unusual RPMs to come from this date. This is 1956D-1MM-016, D and D northwest. The extra mintmark was punched into the tail of the 9 of the date. Considered extremely rare in uncirculated grades, this specimen was found in a circulated roll purchased at a small show. Photo by author.

1956D-1OM-001 shows one of the widest spreads of any mintmark variety in the Lincoln cent series, and is especially unusual because it is an OMM displaying an S between the 1 and 9 of the date. Photo by author.

Look very closely and you should be able to pick out a faint shape of an S mintmark to the east of the D on this example of 1956D-1OM-002. The "horn" sticking out of the lower right portion of the D is the bottom of the S. Photo by author.

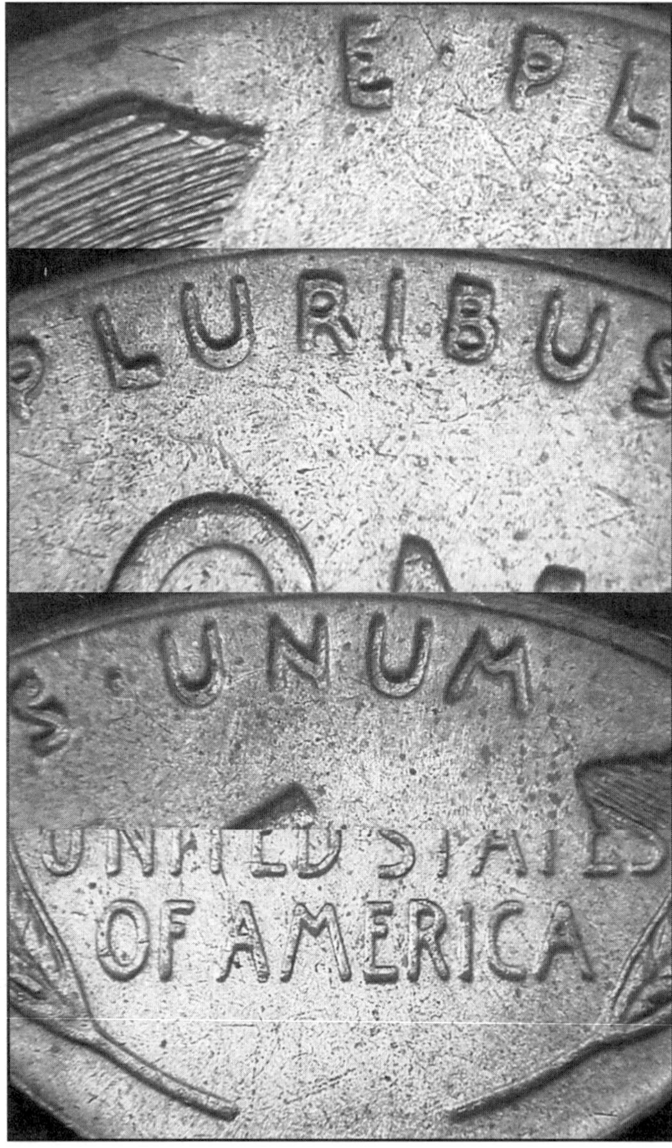

1956P-1DR-001 shows very nice class 6 doubling on the wheat stalks, the motto, and on the tops of the letters of ONE. This is the only class 6 reverse die currently known for 1956 plain cents. Photos by author.

1957

Another banner year for Lincoln cent production, the Denver Mint once again produced over one billion coins. This increase was in part due to cent shortages at banks across the country, and in part due to the lack of a facility minting coins in California. The Philadelphia Mint ran somewhat short on business strike production, minting just over half the amount they made last year, but proof set production skyrocketed. For the first time ever, there were over one million proof sets made.

Quality of 1957 cents is generally good. Fully struck GEM specimens are rather common. However, a vast majority lack the sharpness required for the highest grades. Because of slight strike softness throughout the year, the extremely lofty grades (MS-67 and higher) are scarce and command a nice premium.

Doubled dies and repunched mintmarks are rather common this year, and there are a number of nice examples, although none are major. Watch the area around LIBERTY for doubling on the obverse, especially on the Denver minted cents. There are at least half a dozen different dies carrying such doubling. Doubled eyelids are prolific this year as well, with half a dozen or more known dies existing. Doubled die reverses, mainly class 6, show up on Philadelphia minted cents more so than the Denver minted cents.

Many coins from this year also exhibit master die doubling that is mainly visible in GOD of the motto. The doubling shows as a minor spread on the bottom edge of these letters, especially the D.

Repunched mintmarks are quite numerous this year, with over 50 different dies known. Many of them are minor, but there are a few really nice ones in the lower die numbers. One such RPM also exhibits a doubled die that shows in LIBERTY as described above.

Master die doubling shows on the bottom of the D of GOD on this 1957-D cent.

Die cracks and die breaks are also rather common this year — a number of CUD die breaks and BIE errors are known. The BIE gets its name from the appearance of an I between the B and E of LIBERTY, which was caused by a die break. Machine doubling is also very common this year as are small die chips and breaks in and around the date. None of these errors are scarce, and they do not command much premium value.

Die breaks in LIBERTY are common for this year. These examples are called "BIE" errors because they appear to have an "I" between the B and E. Photos by Bob Piazza.

1957D-1MM-003 shows a nice south spread, but if you look closely it also shows a downward hook off the top right of the mintmark creating a third, east spread. Photo by author.

This is a dual die variety, 1957D-1DO-002 that shows a nice spread in GOD and LIBERTY, and 1957D-1MM-005 that shows a nice south spread on the mintmark. This is one of two dies known for 1957-D that show both a doubled die obverse and a repunched mintmark. Photos by author.

1957P-1DO-002 shows a nice example of class 6 distended hub doubling. Note the concave outer edges to the first few letters of LIBERTY, and the extra thickness in the motto and date. Note also the die break inside the lower B of LIBERTY. This is a die marker for this die but adds no special value of its own since this anomaly is common for this era. Coin submitted by John Morgan, photos by author.

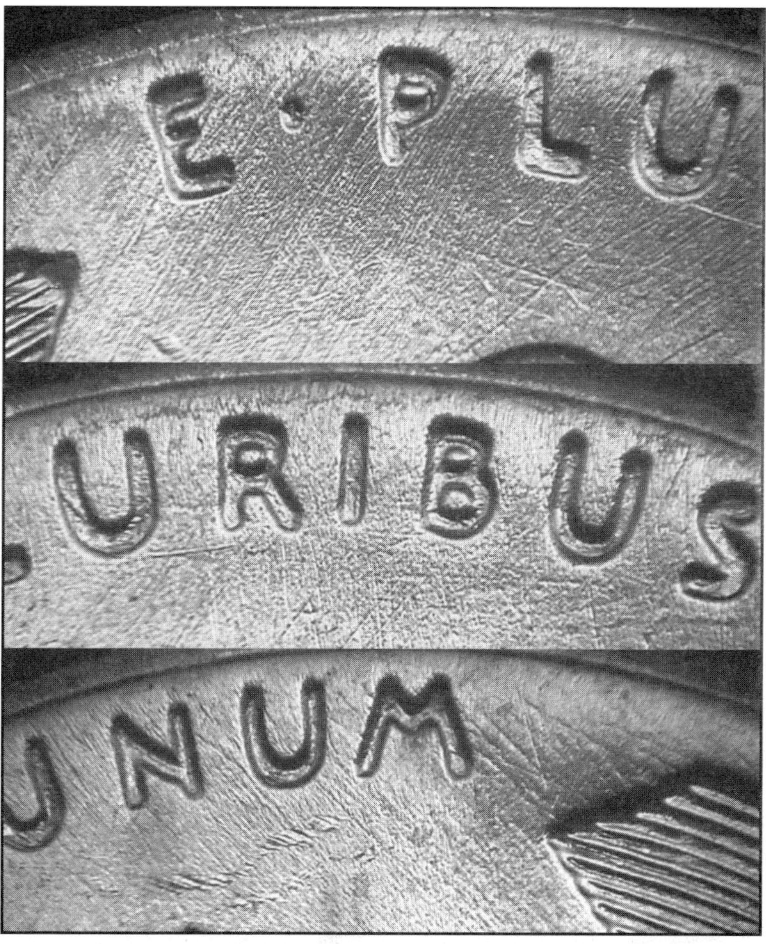

1957P-1DR-001 shows the typical type of reverse hub doubling for this era. It is a class 2 + 6 spread showing extra thickness with a separation line in most of the letters of the motto and both wheat stalks. There are nearly half a dozen such dies for the reverse of 1957 cents. Photos by author.

1957P-1DR-005P is a rather minor example of what a class 2 doubled die reverse looks like on a proof cent. Doubled dies such as this one are found on most years of proof cents from 1954 onward. Photos by author.

1958

The last year of the wheat cent reverse saw production decrease due to a national recession. Cents were only minted a few months of the year at the Philadelphia Mint, which is a turn from the usual 10-12 month run they would typically have. Proof mintage dropped as well, also likely due to the recession. Quality of the cents minted this year is generally good, although a large number of coins were struck with worn out dies. Finding fully struck GEM cents with early die state details can be a challenge.

Doubled dies tend to be on the light side this year. Very few are known outside of the still rather common doubled eyelid cents. One very strong doubled die is known on 1958 plain business strike cents, but to date there are still fewer than half a dozen known specimens of this die variety. This makes it one of the rarest of all stronger doubled dies in the Lincoln cent series. It is highly unlikely that one would pop up in a roll search.

Master die doubling shows up in the 8 of the date this year. The spread is rather minor, but this one has caught a number of collectors thinking it is a normal doubled die. The doubling differs slightly in appearance from die to die depending on the condition of the doubling on the working hub at the time the die was created. These are very common and do not warrant any premium value.

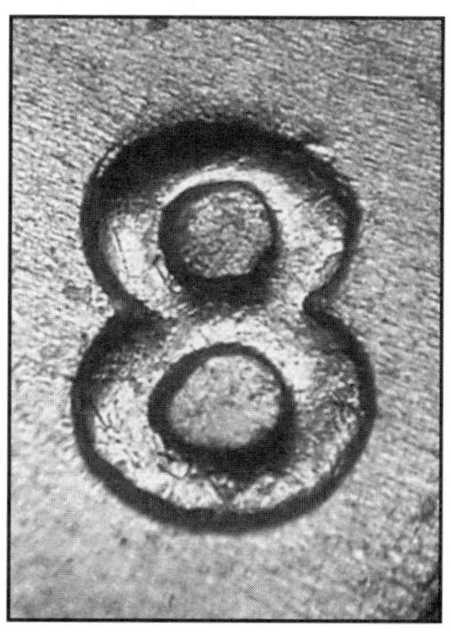

Master die doubling shows as a thin curve on the upper left part of the 8, and the master die gouge on the top right corner of the 8 that is commonly but mistakenly referred to as a 7 digit.

Another anomaly that was originally listed as a 1958 over 7 has since been disproven, and most experts on the topic agree. The "nub" on the top right part of the 8, and the occasional diagonal lines running through the 8 are die gouges created by the reduction lathe at the time the master hub was created. This supposed 8 over 7 shows on most 1958 cents and is not an over date.

Repunched mintmarks are numerous this year. Some of them are rather nice, but the majority of them are minor split serif RPMs with little premium value. The nicest RPM from 1958 and arguably the oddest RPM of the entire series shows parts of five different mintmark punches ranging from the lower vest to touching the primary mintmark. This repunched mintmark is considered quite scarce and valuable.

Die cracks, breaks, and other minor anomalies such as machine doubling are rather common this year. Expect a wide assortment of these minor errors, but don't expect them to be worth very much. The market of interest for these is quite small.

1958D-1MM-001 shows a very nice spread to the south and yet another punch as an upper split serif. Photo by author.

1958D-1DO-001 shows nice class 1 rotated hub doubling above the 9 of the date and just below the B of LIBERTY. Doubling under the B of LIBERTY tends to be somewhat common this year. At least three dies are known to have this doubling for 1958 and none like them have been reported to date in any surrounding year. Photos by author.

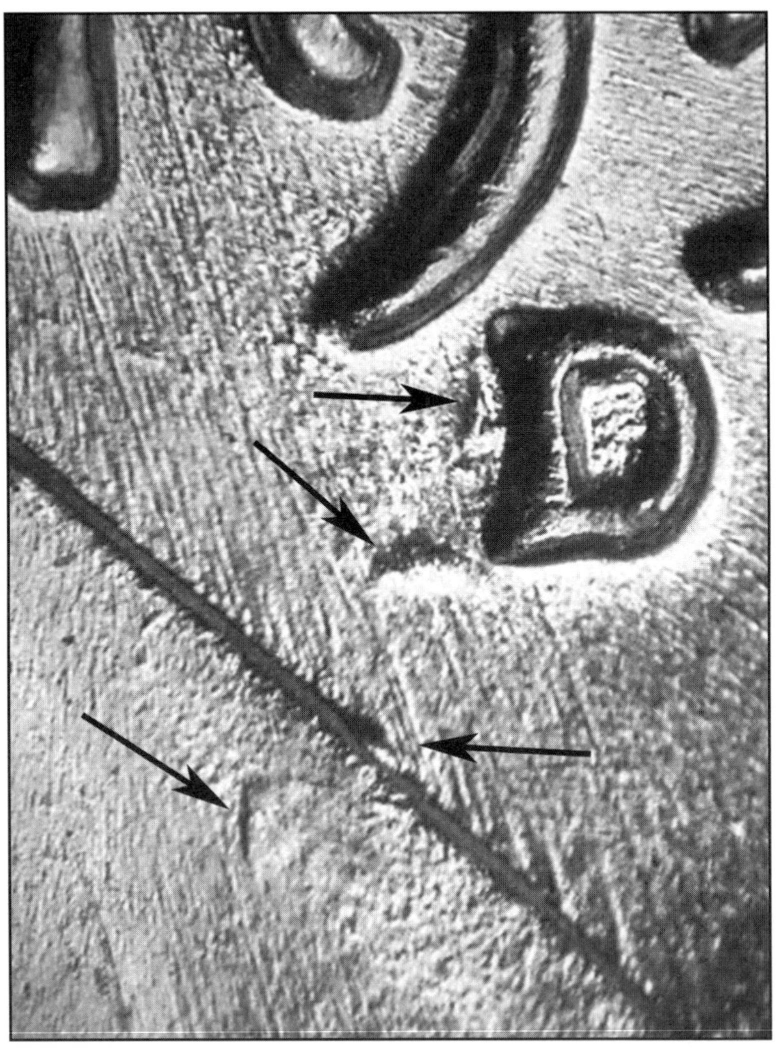

1958D-1MM-021 is listed as having five mintmark punchings. All of the stray marks match the general shape of a D mintmark, and all of them would have to come from separate punchings. With this being the case, this RPM has more notable separated punchings than any other RPM in the Lincoln cent series. Photos by author.

8 | CHRONOLOGY OF THE LINCOLN CENT

THE MEMORIAL
REVERSE:
1959-Date

Overview

In 1909 Abraham Lincoln's bust first appeared on the cent obverse to commemorate his 100th birthday. From that time to 1959, another half century passed. Americans had grown accustomed to their Lincoln cents with the wheat stalks on the reverse, but in January 1959, that era in our coinage was to be written and sealed in history.

On December 20, 1958, President Dwight D. Eisenhower authorized a change of the Lincoln cent reverse to one designed by Assistant Engraver Frank Gasparro. This left just enough time to prepare the dies and have them ready to commence striking on the second day of January, two short weeks later.

The new reverse design, perhaps inspired by Jefferson's memorial introduced twenty years earlier on the nickel's reverse, was to bear the likeness of the Lincoln Memorial in Washington, D.C. The design was clean and fresh, bearing all the same lettering as the wheat reverse cent, yet in different positions and with a different letter style.

Since 1959, more memorial reverse cents have been minted than all other cent types in the history of our nation. In fact, over 400 billion Lincoln memorial cents have been minted, more than any other single coin design in world history.

Soon the Lincoln cent will be 100 years old, and the memorial reverse will be half that age. What is to come of the 'penny', now so diminished as a medium of exchange by time and inflation? What will happen to this seemingly familiar mainstay in commerce that, in reality, the general public knows so little about it? Only time can tell.

1959

The 150th anniversary of the birth of Abraham Lincoln prompted the U.S. Mint to change the reverse of the Lincoln cent to show the likeness of the Lincoln Memorial building standing in Washington D.C. Mint engraver Frank Gasparro, who incidentally was born in 1909 — the same year as the first release of the Lincoln cent — designed this new reverse.

Changing from the wheat cent reverse to the memorial cent reverse was smooth — except in one case. A single example of a 1959-D wheat reverse cent was discovered in California in 1986 and has since been examined and deemed genuine by a number of authorities. Others, however, are not quite so sure the coin can be genuine. The U.S. Mint insisted that they changed the die pairs together, and that no 1959 cents could have been struck with wheat reverses. Whether a clandestine fantasy piece by a mint employee or a true error, the coin still exists, and no others have been found and reported to date. It is still worth the effort to be casually observant of the possibility that more could exist.

Doubled dies this year are rather few and are scattered as to where to look for them. Some affect the date, some affect LIBERTY only, and some are on the reverse. There is no particular pattern to follow except to look at photos of the known dies and hope for the best. 1959 doubled dies are at least difficult to locate.

Repunched mintmarks, on the other hand, are quite numerous. Over 50 different dies are known, but many of them are rather minor. There is one oddity to mention for this date — a 1959-D cent with what appears to be the lower part of a D punched inside the last 9 of the date. This anomaly has been given a die number by some and rejected as die damage by others, and with at least some merit — there is damage near the rim on the die just outside the date that somewhat matches the reported punch inside the 9. This one has to be left to the collector to decide. Coppercoins.com has it listed as a repunched mintmark until further evidence dictates otherwise.

Overall, 1959 is a fun year to search through, but don't expect very much. The really nice doubled dies and repunched mintmarks are numerous compared to some other years, but the sheer number of surviving coins has spread the nice die varieties thin enough that a person could look through a number of rolls without finding them. Be patient and the gems will eventually surface.

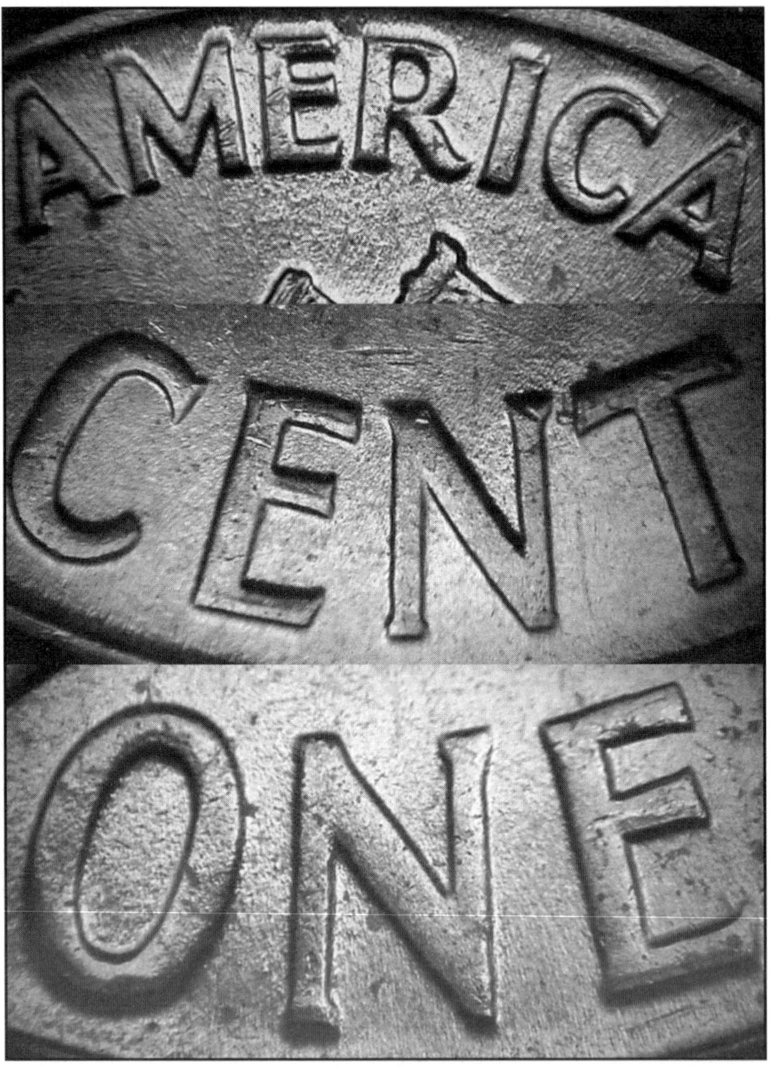

1959P-1DR-001 has the widest spread of any of the known 1959 doubled die reverses. It shows a weak separation and wide extra thickness which is most accurately described by adding classes 2 and 6 together. Photos by author.

Above: *1959D-1DO-001 shows mild extra thickness in the date and motto. This doubled die can be difficult to spot if you do not know the design and the normal thickness of the digits. Photo by author.*

Below: *1959D-1MM-001 shows three mintmarks clustered together. This RPM was the study piece experts used to determine that some die varieties show their attributes better in later die states. This coin shows a near complete curve on the right most punch, but earlier die state coins show an incomplete curve. This is the result of die wear. Photo by author.*

Two of the nicer and less common RPMs for 1959-D are 1959D-1MM-005 (above) and 1959D-1MM-007 (below). Both of these RPMs were found in roll searches, but as the supply of unsearched rolls dries up, these are becoming increasingly diffuclt to find. Photos by author.

This is 1959D-1MM-021, listed as an RPM because of what appears to be the vertical bar of a D mintmark punch inside the last 9 of the date. It is contested as an RPM by some because it is believed that the proposed extra D punch is an extension of the damage near the rim outside the date. Some collectors follow the damage theory and others believe it is a true RPM and trade coins displaying this anomaly at $20-$30 per uncirculated copy. This author believes this die to exhibit an RPM, however will leave it to the collector to decide for themselves. Photo by author.

1959P-1DO-004 shows nice class 2 distorted hub doubling in LIBERTY, but does not show doubling anywhere else on the design. Photo by author.

1960

Extremely high production numbers and a large number of bags and rolls saved this year have kept the 1960 cent relatively low in value. One thing that has helped the market for bulk 1960 cents is the extremely high number of die varieties that have been reported. To date, a "complete" set of all known doubled dies, repunched mintmarks, and date size differences for 1960 numbers over 200 coins — the most for any year of the Lincoln cent.

Heading off the pack of oddities for this year is a hub change early in the year that involved a slight change in the size of the digits in the date. When the public caught wind of this change, they raced to banks and hoarded mass quantities of cents hoping their investment would turn out to be the "rarity" for the year. Those who ended up with primarily small date bags from Philadelphia came out being the winners. Far fewer small date cents were minted in Philadelphia than large date cents, causing a scarcity that currently sells for a few dollars per coin in uncirculated grades, and over $80 by the roll. Compared to the few cents per coin or $1 per roll for their large date counterpart, that's one heck of a difference!

The date size change also caused another odd problem: the first Lincoln cents minted with two different date sizes on the same coin (save a very odd 1949-S doubled die). These doubled dies are scarce to very rare, and surprisingly are mostly on proof cents. Three different dies are known exhibiting small over large (or vice versa) on proof cents, and a single example is known on Denver minted cents, which incidentally comes with a nice RPM.

Master die doubling is evident inside the upper area of the E and on the end of the center crosslet of the E as shown here.

Master die doubling is also evident this year, showing as light doubling inside the E of WE on most large date variety cents. Expect no premium value for this doubling, as it is very common.

Repunched mintmarks, as described above, are extremely numerous this year, and quite a number of them are very nice as well. In fact, the strongest RPM in the Lincoln cent series was minted this year. Out of the nearly 200 different dies known, nearly 50 of them are very nice, another 50 are minor to moderate, and the remainder are split serif minor RPMs with little premium value. Many of the RPMs for this year are considered rather common, but this is likely because 1960-D cents are among the most searched-through date in the series. Roll prices are low and bags still exist in the hundreds, although they are drying up because of all the die variety hunters who know this is the best year in which you have a good chance to find something interesting.

With the very odd doubled dies, the date size change, and the largest batch of RPMs in the whole series, the remainder of the known doubled dies for this year are completely lackluster. There are a few rather minor doubled die obverses, a number of "bar-L" doubled dies, and a few doubled die reverses worth mentioning.

Die breaks such as those seen here on a 1960-D small date cent are one reason why the Mint changed to the large date hubs. Photo by Bob Piazza

Top: *A small date 1960 cent. Notice that the top of the 9 is parallel to the top of the 1, the 6 is shorter, and the zero in the date is smaller with a smaller center. Photo by author.*

Bottom: *A large date 1960 cent shows that the top of the 9 extends above the top of the 1, the 6 is larger, wider, and more open, and the zero is larger with a larger center. Photo by author.*

The 1960 date size change is the easiest to detect of all the date size changes. Other parts of the design are affected, but much more moderately than the date.

Some Nicer 1960-D RPMs

1960D-1MM-002

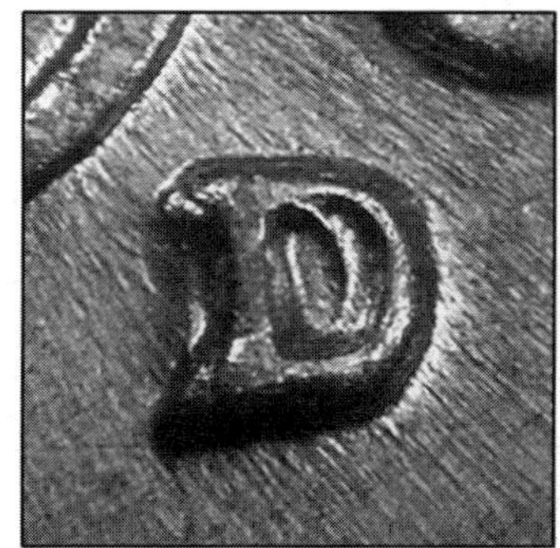

1960D-1MM-003

1960D-1MM-013

1960D-1MM-015

1960D-1MM-021

1960D-1MM-023

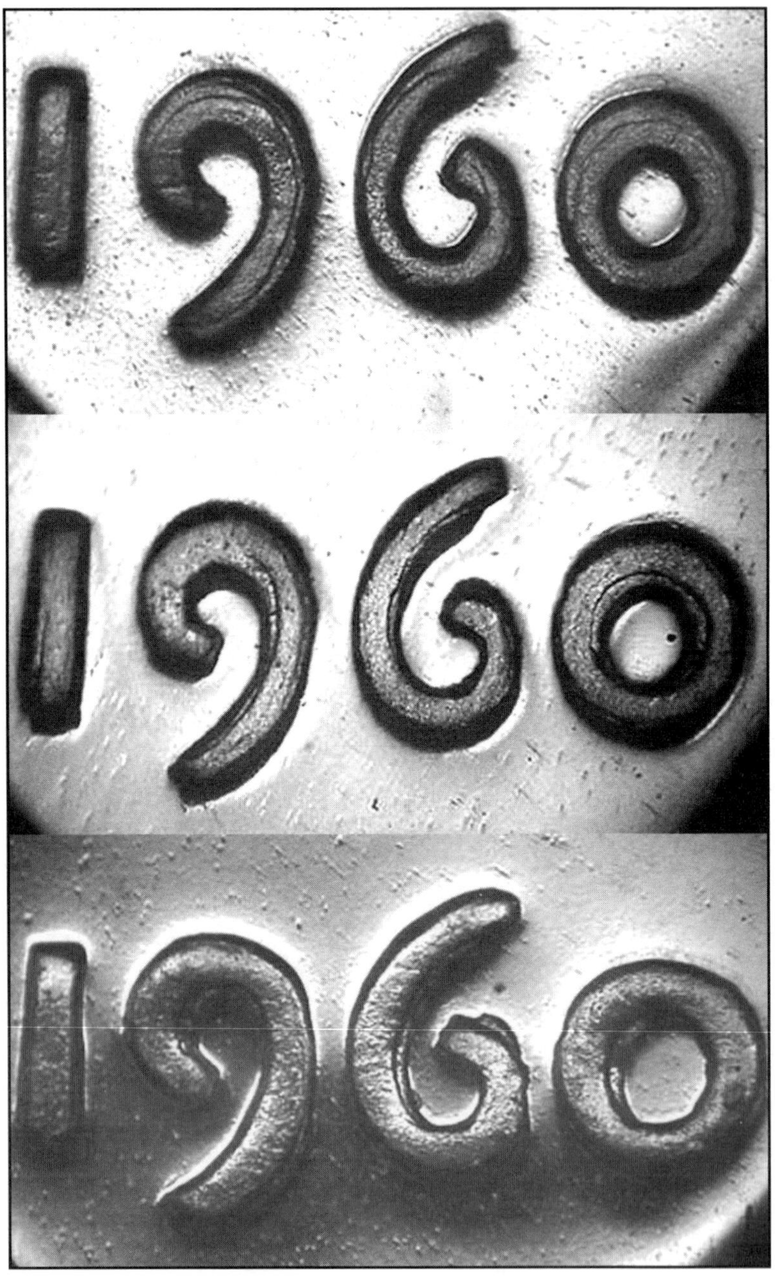

Opposing Page:

Top: *1960P-1DO-002P shows a very nicely detailed small date over large date hubbing. Coin from Joe Yuknalis, photo by author.*

Center: *1960P-1DO-003P shows just the opposite — a large date over a small date. Coin from Joe Yuknalis, photo by author.*

Bottom: *1960P-1DO-004P is a tripled die obverse. It is first a large date over a small date, but also has class 6 doubling in the large date hubbings. Notice the extra thickness in the tail of the 9 of the date. Coin from Joe Yuknalis, photo by author.*

This Page:

1960D-1DO-001 is an especially wild doubled die because it is accompanied by a very nice RPM, 1960D-1MM-100. The doubled die shows a very nice small over large date hubbing, and the RPM shows a very wide and clear spread to the north. Examples of this die are quite valuable, especially in early die state, which does not show the die crack extending southward from the 1 of the date as does the coin photographed. Photo by author.

This is an example of 1960D-1MM-004, one of the scarcest RPMs in modern Lincoln cents. The secondary mintmark is visible as two short lines protruding from the upper serif of the primary mintmark. Only known up to early mid-die state, examples of this die are rarely offered for sale, and when they are, uncirculated specimens typically sell for over $75. Photo by Richard S. Cooper.

1960D-1MM-001 is the most visible example of a repunched mintmark in the Lincoln cent series. Examples of this die are more common than some other 1960-D RPMs, but because of the extreme nature of this RPM it sells for $10-$20 in uncirculated grades. Photo by author.

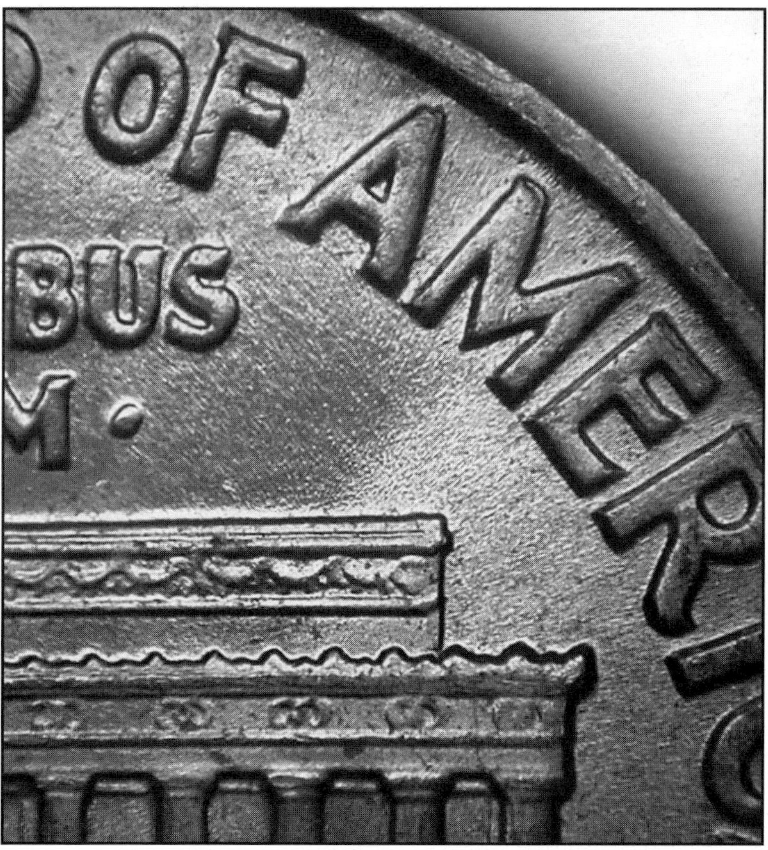

This is 1960P-1DR-002. It shows extreme class 6 hub doubling all over the reverse and is a fantastic example of such doubling on a memorial reverse cent. Unfortunately, however, it is known in all die states including very late die state, thus it is very common. Examples of this die in varying die states are very widespread, limiting its value to under $5 in uncirculated grades. This example is an EDS example. Coin by Frank Baumann, photo by author.

1960D-1DO-002 shows very nice class 1 rotated hub doubling in the motto. This doubled die is quite scarce and typically sells for over $20 for uncirculated examples. Coin by Gene Nichols, photos by author.

1961

For the third year in a row cent production increased at the Mint. With just over 2.5 billion cents produced, there is no shortage of 1961 cents. Uncirculated rolls and bags are plentiful, but expect a number of them to be dull or spotted from poor storage. Very late die state coins are also quite common, especially for Denver minted cents. Proof set production topped 3 million sets this year, but expect full cameo strikes to be rather scarce. Full rolls of 1961 proof cents are easy to obtain for usually under $20 per roll.

Past listings of large and small date cents for 1961 have been disproved as a result of die polishing. Discount any differences in thickness and apparent size of the digits of the date on this year's cents, as they are the result of die over polishing to remove clash marks. All 1961-cent hubs were made with the same design.

Doubled dies are typically minor this year, except for proof issues. Doubled eyelids, bar-L cents, and minor doubling in LIBERTY tend to make up the majority of doubled dies for the business strike cents, and most of the known examples are on Philadelphia minted coins. As for proofs, some really nice doubled die reverses have been reported, but very few obverse doubled dies are known.

Master die doubling exists again this year. It shows as minor doubling toward the center of the design in GOD of the motto. This doubling is sometimes combined with other doubling, so be mindful of that. Do not discount every coin with this doubling as master die doubling only.

Repunched mintmarks are numerous again this year, although the number of different dies reported is half

Master die douibling on a 1961-D cent. This doubling is common and has no value. Photo by author.

that of 1960, and many of them are rather minor. Quite a number of 1961 RPMs are impressive, however, but only one is as impressive as the nicest ones from 1960. That one is a D over a horizontal D punch that is rotated nearly 90 degrees clockwise. This RPM is considered somewhat common, but because it is unusual in nature it typically brings $10-$15 in uncirculated grades.

Die cracks and small die breaks are common this year as well, with many of them on the head, in LIBERTY, and on either side of the memorial building on the reverse. These have typically very little collector interest and do not warrant any premium value.

Although mintmark varieties are not as numerous as last year, they are still very easy to find in rolls. Doubled dies are a bit scarcer, but they also tend to show up with minimal effort. Taking into account the inexpensive prices for rolls and bags, 1961 offers a nice choice for variety hunters.

1961D-1MM-001 shows one of the nicest known "horizontal" RPMs. One can readily see the nearly 90 degree clockwise rotation of the secondary mintmark. Photo by author.

1961P-1DO-002 shows mild class 6 doubling in the date and motto. It also shows the master die doubling described in the text. Photos by author.

1961P-1DO-003 shows very minor but very clear doubling on the top of the L and I of LIBERTY. This die also shows the master die doubling described in the text. Photo by author.

1961P-1DR-002P shows a very nice example of the class 2 distorted hub doubling that is rather common for proof cents of this era. These are not difficult to find as a group, but finding individual dies can be quite a challenge. Most dies such as this one sell for $25-$50 in PR65-RD or better condition. Photos by author.

1962

Since the reintroduction of tin in the Lincoln cent composition in 1947 had been less than one percent of the total composition of the cent, it was a rather insignificant part of the overall metal used to strike the coins. By 1962 the total amount of tin in a cent was barely enough to detect under the most sensitive scales. Congress passed a law removing the tin from the cent altogether in September. The amount of zinc in the cent's composition was slightly increased and production continued through the end of the year. Although both metallic compositions exist for 1962 cents, the difference is undetectable so collector interest in attempting to find the difference has been non-existent.

High mintage is still the rule in 1962; nearly 2.5 billion cents were struck again this year. Again, uncirculated bags and rolls are quite plentiful and can be found at price levels that are at or below double face value. Proof sets are again very common as are rolls of proof cents, again at $20 or less per roll. Most of these are the result of dismantled sets in which the best coins were removed and submitted for grading, so what remained for rolls were typically the coins that were not cameo or were not of high enough grade to warrant slab fees.

Because most proof sets were dismantled for grade only, the rolls that remain are usually loaded with doubled dies. I have never failed to find at least one doubled die in every roll of 1962 proof cents purchased, and have found as many as 30 in a single roll. Doubled dies for 1962 proof cents number over 30 counting obverse and reverse together, with the majority of these showing in the date. At one time these obverse doubled dies were considered so plentiful they were initially believed to be master die doubling, but upon further review they were found to have a number of different spreads (which would be impossible for master die doubling), so they were broken down and listed as separate doubled dies.

Repunched mintmarks are not nearly as numerous as in previous years. Although there are a number of different dies to be found, most of them are minor. While searching for RPMs, watch for a problem that occurred with the mintmark punch this year that somewhat resembles the broken punch of 1952. This one, however, shows a dent or dimple

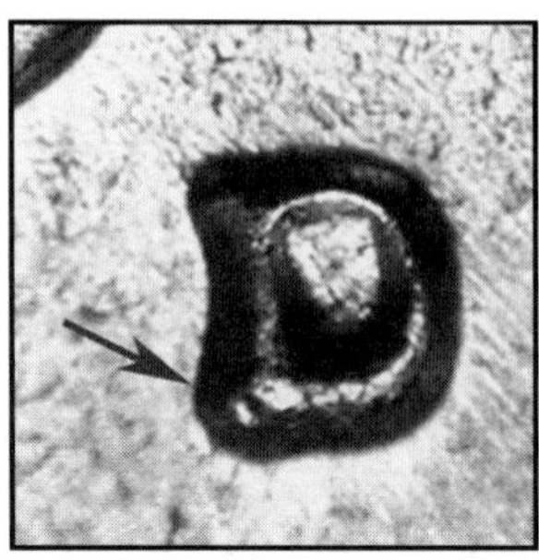

This 1962-D mintmark shows evidence of a damaged punch. Photo by author.

in the lower serif that many collectors have mistaken for RPMs.

Cents from 1962 have been reported in the past as having been from two different designs, something rather unclear having to do with the front of the hairline and how it meets the forehead. Disregard such claims. Any difference noted in Lincoln's bust is a result of die polishing and not of a design change. All 1962 business strike cents were minted from dies created with the same design.

Although the general spread of die varieties for this year is rather lackluster and very few dies stick out as being even moderately interesting, there are still enough of them in quantity to sufficiently populate rolls. This makes the rolls at least interesting if not occasionally valuable. Although not rated as one of the top memorial years to dig through (except for proofs), they are still worth the buy at the current market price.

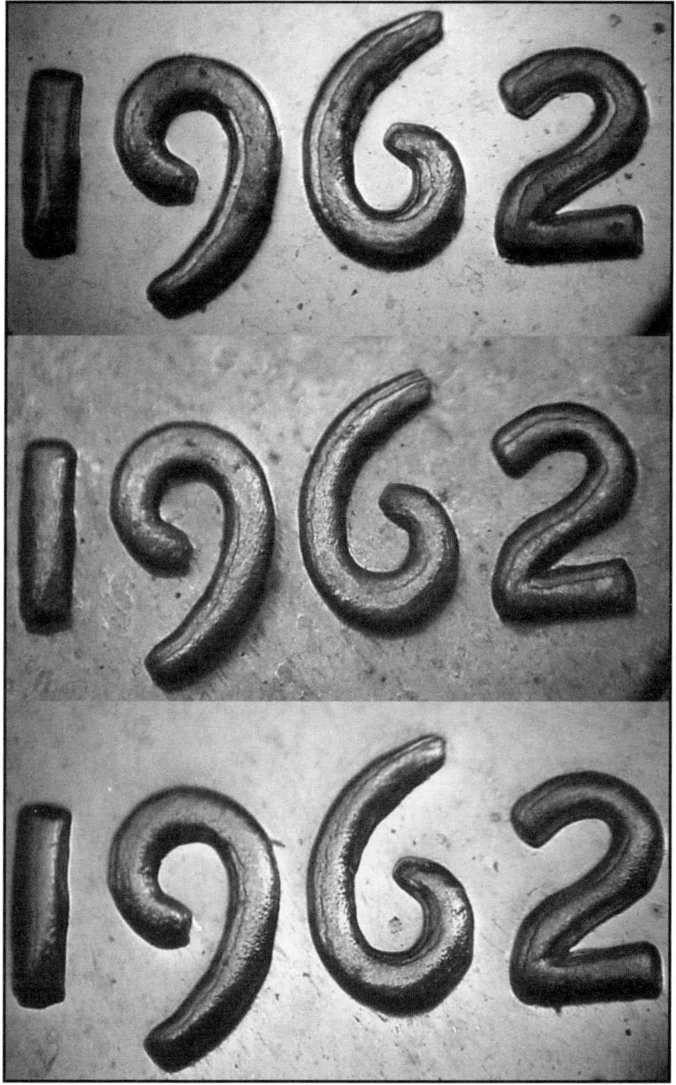

In order from top to bottom, these are 1962P-1DO-001P, 002P, and 003P. All three of these coins show similar doubling in the date, although their spreads are all slightly different. Finding proof strike 1962 cents with doubling in the date is common, but each individual die is rather scarce. Photos by author.

The same form of doubling that is quite common on 1962 proof cents is actually quite scarce on the business strike cents. This is 1962P-1DO-020. It shows very nice doubling in the date and in TRUST. Photos by author.

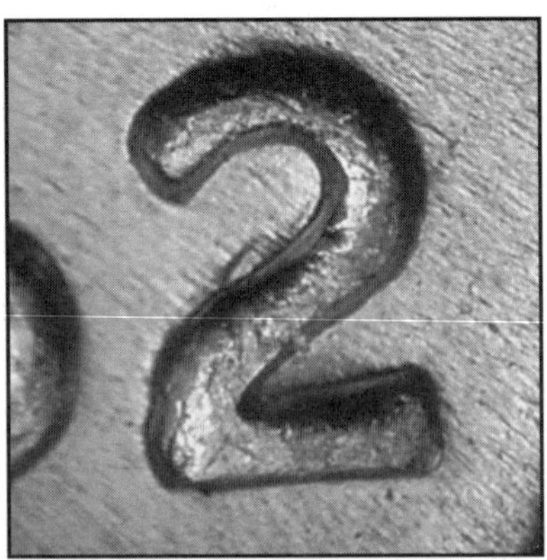

1962P-1DO-021 shows remnants of a high 2 inside the normal 2 of the date. Although far less impressive than other doubled dies of this date, this die can be difficult to detect if you do not know what to look for. Photo by author.

1962P-1DO-023 shows a nice spread in the date and LIBERTY, with a very mild spread in the last two letters of TRUST. This is just one example of many for this date that show this kind of doubling (class 2 distorted hub doubling), but this one is one of the stronger examples for business strike cents. Coin by Roger Anderson, photos by author.

1963

The quantity of 1963 cents minted rivals that of the past few years with very little change. With that being said, availability of rolls and bags is still very high; this is the lowest priced year of uncirculated Lincoln cent rolls in history, with dealer trade prices at barely over face value. The positive side to this is that it provides a treasure trove for die variety hunters at a very low price. Proof set production was comparable to previous years, and full cameo cents are a little more common than in 1962.

Doubled dies are quite plentiful this year. A return of the doubled eyelids and a heavy increase in bar-L cents this year make 1963 cents a nice choice for those wanting to pick up a pile of minor doubled dies, but don't forget to check the reverse of those coins. A number of reverse doubled dies have been reported on 1963 cents, many of them on proof issues. One particular Denver minted doubled die with high collector interest shows a normal 3 hubbed over a partially removed very low 3 in the date. These are uncommon and typically sell for $10-15 in uncirculated grades.

1963D-1DO-003 shows a nicely tripled bar-L type doubled die. These are class 8, tilted hub doubled dies. Notice also that this particular die doubling shows on the bottom of the I and B as well. Photo by author.

Repunched mintmarks remain on the status quo with 1962. Over 20 of them are known, but most are quite minor. Also like 1962, the same dimple shows in the lower serif of the mintmark on many examples.

Because of inexpensive roll prices and a rather large number of doubled dies, 1963 comes recommended as a good year for die variety hunters.

Doubling such as that seen here on 1963D-1DR-001 is quite common on Philadelphia minted cents of this era, but is rather unusual for Denver minted cents. Class 2 doubling shows on the outer edges of much of the lettering, and is usually stronger on the lower half of the design. Photos by author.

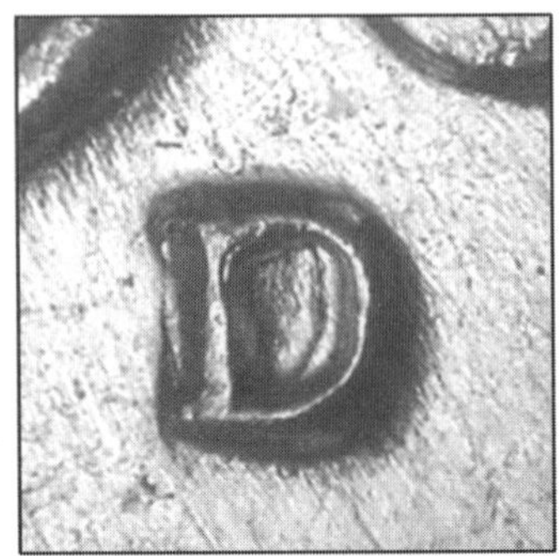

1963D-1MM-001

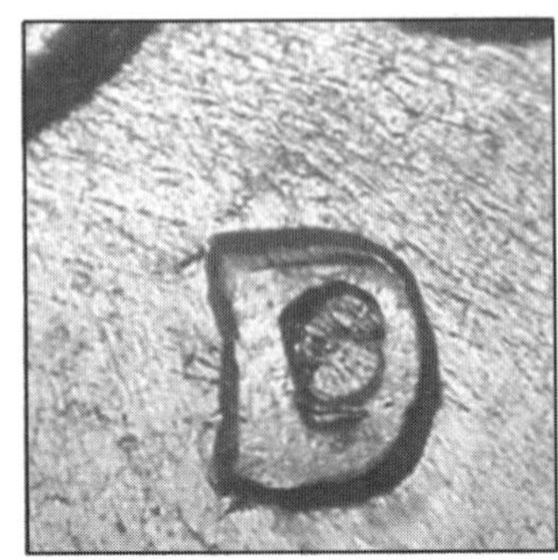

1963D-1MM-004

1963D-1MM-006

1963D-1MM-009

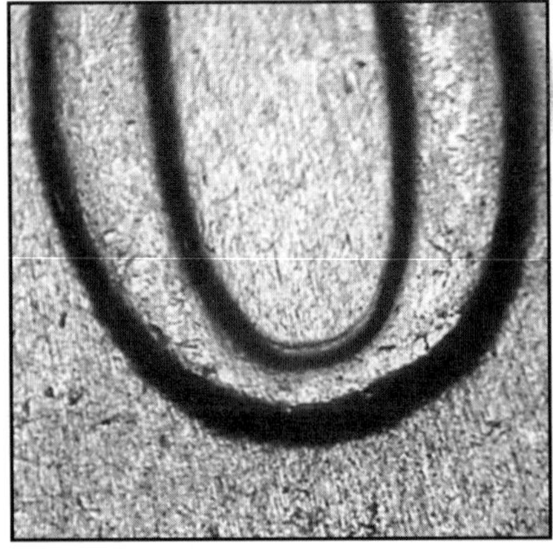

Doubling such as that seen here inside the O of ONE on the reverse of a 1963-P cent is master die doubling and should be dismissed. It exists on a number of cents ranging from 1960-1964. Photo by author.

These photos are both of 1963D-1DO-001. The top photo shows an early die state example on which the doubling shows on the lower part of the 3 as well as in the center. The lower photo is of an LDS example on which the doubling only shows in the center part of the 3. Top photo by author, bottom photo by Bob Piazza.

1964

A dramatic increase in overall production this year caused 1964 cents to be some of the most available Lincoln cents in history. Thousands of rolls and bags are readily available at very modest premiums, and rolls of proof 1964 cents are plentiful at $15-$20 per roll. Like with 1963, this is a good omen for die variety hunters.

1964 marks the climax of Lincoln cent doubled die production. Over 100 different doubled dies are known. Although most of them are minor, there are quite a few that are very nice. In fact some of them are nearly visible to the naked eye. One such die is on the reverse of 1964 Philadelphia minted cents and shows very strong class 1 rotated hub doubling. Its main pick up point is in the word STATES. A large number of proof cents also show hub doubling, most of them are on the reverse as well. The vast majority of all 1964 doubled die reverse cents are class 2, distorted hub doubling, showing mainly on the outside edges of the letters in ONE CENT or the designer's initials.

The 4 of the date on many 1964 business strike and proof cents has been the cause of controversy in that many examples show very minor doubling above the crosslet on the far right side of the digit. While these have been considered individual doubled dies in the past, it is my opinion that most of these were caused by either a doubled master die or a doubled working hub. Far too many of them exist for this anomaly to have occurred on each individual die involved. These should not, however, be confused with true doubled dies that show stronger doubling in the same area.

The crosslet of the 4 shows very minor doubling on many 1964 cents. Photo by author.

Repunched mintmarks are mixed this year. There are over two dozen different dies known, however, most of them are quite minor. The known dies that are not minor are very nice ones - feast or famine. The mintmark punch was changed this year to a slightly larger, sharper serif version. This new style of mintmark shows very minor split serifs on a large number of dies that are too minor to warrant attention, causing confusion for those who are trying to collect and catalog every RPM they find under high magnification. The general rule is that in order to give minor RPMs die numbers, they have to have enough spread to photograph under 30 power magnification and be visible enough to see with 16 power under normal lighting conditions. Many of these extremely minor 1964-D RPMs do not meet these criteria and thus are not listed.

Overall, 1964 is an inexpensive year for collectors with extremely high mintage survivability in uncirculated condition. There are a very high number of doubled dies to search for, and repunched mintmarks are easy to locate as well. All of this together makes 1964 a very good year for die variety hunters.

This photo of the lower NT of CENT on 1964D-1DR-004 shows the most typical type of doubling one is likely to find. This is class 2 distorted hub doubling and it has a spread toward the center of the design. Notice how the lower extremities are doubled all the way across. Photo by author.

1964P-1DR-001 shows a very nice counterclockwise class 1 rotated spread. This is one of the nicest reverse doubled dies in the Lincoln cent series and is by far the best example for this date. These coins are quite scarce even though the die minted enough coins to reach late die state. They typically sell for $30-$50 in uncirculated grades. Photos by author.

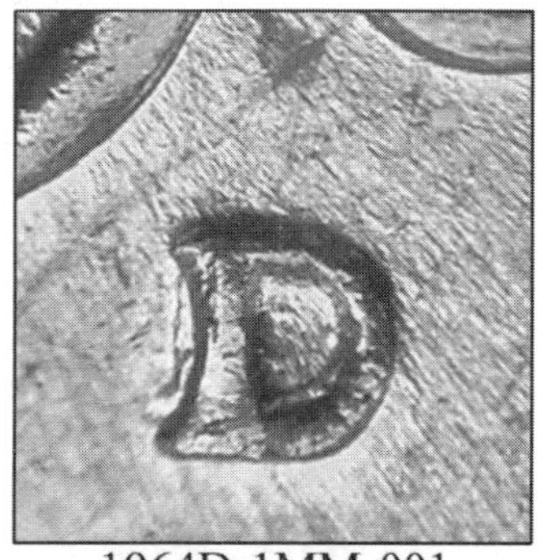

1964D-1MM-001

1964D-1MM-002

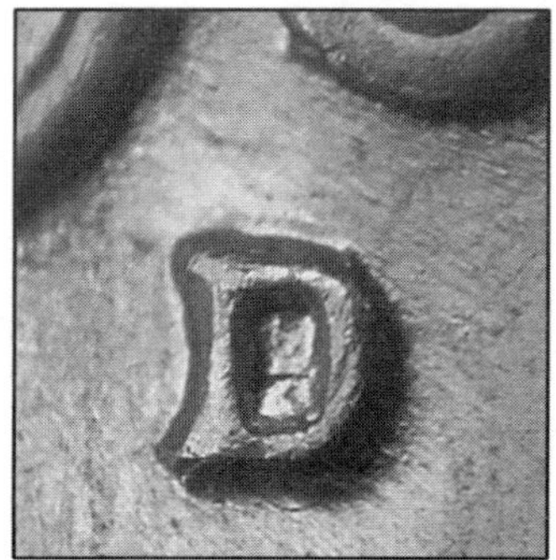

1964D-1MM-004

1964D-1MM-009

Above*: Some of the nicer repunched mintmarks for 1964-D. Altogether there are nearly two dozen different dies for this date. Photos by author.*

Next Page*: Very common occurrences on cents of this era. From top to bottom, machine doubling, a large die break at the right eave of the memorial building, and two photos of extreme die wear. Photos by author.*

1965-1967

The change from silver to clad coinage for dimes, quarters, and half dollars (which were still 40 percent silver until 1971) at the close of 1964 left the Mint racing to produce enough of the new coins to survive the demand. By the end of 1965, it had fallen so far behind that 1965 cents were minted through the first quarter of 1966, and changes at the Mint forced them to nearly completely abandon quality.

A decision by the Mint to foil speculator hoarding left 1965 cents (and the two subsequent years) without mintmarks on the cents and left me without much to say about them. Repunched mintmarks are impossible without mintmarks, and it seems the boon of doubled dies experienced just the year before had completely dried up. Of all three years combined, there are a total of three known doubled dies - a single 1965 obverse, a single 1966 obverse, and a rather nice 1966 reverse. No die varieties are known on 1967 cents.

Production in 1965 dropped to levels that had not been experienced since before the memorial reverse was introduced. Both operating mints produced a combined total of just fewer than 1.5 billion coins. 1966 and 1967 saw steady increases, however in neither of those years were there quite the number of cents minted as the Denver Mint alone in 1964. Even with the lower production these three years, fully struck GEM quality cents are elusive. Oddly enough, 1967 saw the highest production of cents out of these three years, but currently trades at the highest price per uncirculated roll and is the most difficult to find. This is likely due to a general collector disinterest in the coins minted during this era.

For the first time since 1949, the Mint did not produce proof sets in any of these three years. They opted instead to mint what was referred to as the special mint set. These sets, minted by the newly reopened San Francisco Mint, were typically lower in quality than the proof sets minted in recent years because the coins were struck on normal cent planchets with polished dies, and although they did not suffer bagging, they were not handled with the care that proof coins had been handled with at the Philadelphia Mint.

Although a couple of decent surprises are known to lurk in 1966 cents for the very patient hunter, these three years represent some of the least interesting years of the entire series.

One final subject of note is that the 5 digit of the date on 1965 cents has a notch in the center where the curve meets the upright. 1965 was the only use of this style of five, which has caused some confusion among collectors. These have been reported and sold as doubled dies in the past, but are a normal part of the design.

This 1965 cent shows a notch in the center left part of the digit that is common to all cents of this year. Photo by author.

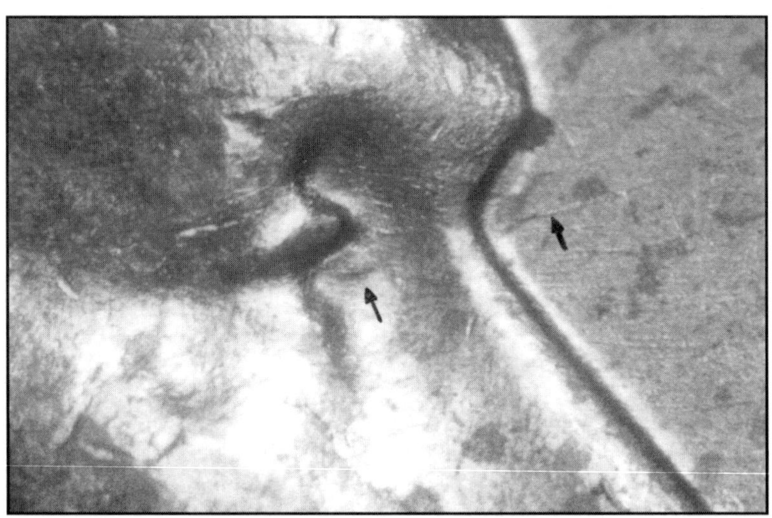

This doubled eyelid is listed in the Crawford Files as 1965 CDDO-001 and is the only known doubled die for 1965 cents. The arrow to the right points to one of the die markers, a die scratch leading northeast from the bridge of the nose. Photo by Billy Crawford.

1968

A return to mintmarks and proof sets shows that the Mint was over their problematic period of catching up to a coinage shortage and changing metallic content of most of the circulating coins. Mintage returned to pre-1965 levels with one major change — the San Francisco Mint's distinguishable S mintmark returned not only to business strike cents for the first time since 1955, but to proof coinage as well. Special collector sets had been minted in San Francisco without mintmarks since 1965, and with the lifting of the mintmark ban in 1967, the Mint decided to once again use the familiar mintmark of the west coast mint. This created the first ever U.S. issued proof coins bearing mintmarks.

Doubled dies and repunched mintmarks are sparsely distributed this year, although some of the known examples are very nice. This means collectors are far less likely to find die varieties on 1968 cents, but the ones they do find are usually very nice. Most sought after is a strong class 5 pivoted hub doubled die reverse found on some 1968-D cents.

One important thing to be very mindful of when searching through 1968 cents is that machine doubling is extremely common on this year's cents. Very deep devices on the coins could be one of the causes. However, a design change in 1969 did not stop the onslaught of machine doubled coins, so deep devices cannot be the only reason. It is believed that overall quality control was lacking during this era, which would answer for many of the machine doubling problems exhibited on cents from 1968 through 1971.

Another detrimental feature of 1968 cents is the fact that the master design used for all 1968 cents is the same one that had been used for decades on the Lincoln cent and it was definitely showing its age. The details on the bust had become mushy and the motto merges with the rim on typically struck cents. This is a very common occurrence that holds most of the coins to a low GEM status at best.

1968D-1DR-001 (Crawford Files 1968D CDDR-001) shows a very nice class 5 pivoted hub doubled clockwise spread. This doubled die is very rare and commands a hefty premium. Photos by Billy Crawford.

1968D-1DO-001 shows a very nice class 2 spread toward the edge of the design in the date and motto. Photos by author.

Machine Damage Doubling is very common for 1968 cents. Above, notice that the mintmark is doubled with the date, which never occurs with doubled dies. Notice also that the doubling is flattened and has a sharp edge. Below, the same effect shows on the reverse of a 1968-D cent. Notice in this example how the machine doubling is confined to the outer lettering. It is common for machine doubling to affect some areas of the design and not other areas. Photos by author.

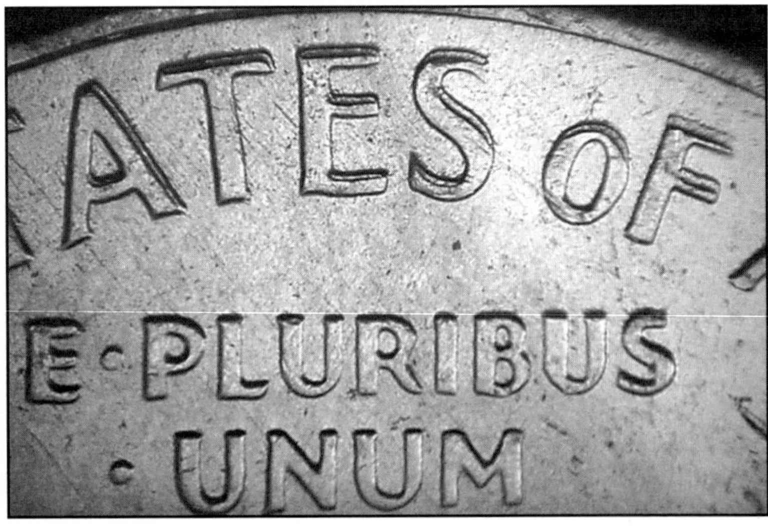

1969

Because the design of the Lincoln cent had grown old and needed refreshing, the Mint re-engraved the design and created a new design engraving for this year. The design more closely resembles the original Brenner design created in 1909 than the coins minted in recent years. The reverse was also changed but is much less apparent than the nearly bald obverse of 1968 to the redone obverse of 1969.

Slightly lower mintage and a high demand for top-grade coins has pushed 1969 Philadelphia Mint rolls upward in value. Rolls of these cents can be somewhat difficult to locate. Denver and San Francisco minted cents remain at levels around three times face value and are plentiful. Bags are not quite as common as in previous years, but do exist.

Doubled dies are extremely limited this year, but one doubled die for 1969-S cents more than makes up for the loss of having no known Philadelphia minted examples and only one doubled die obverse known for Denver cents. The 1969-S doubled die has been listed in guides since its discovery, but very few examples have surfaced, making it one of the most valuable of all Lincoln cent doubled dies. Prices for this monster have risen past $10,000 for uncirculated examples in recent years, and it is likely that these prices will only climb as time goes on.

Repunched mintmarks are also limited this year in comparison to the early 60's. Although nearly two-dozen different RPMs are known for this date, most of them are minor. Because all 1969 RPMs are elusive and difficult to find, most of them command nice premium values of around $5 each in choice uncirculated condition.

As with 1968 cents, this year's cents are very common for displaying machine doubling to some degree. Because the major doubled die for 1969-S has been listed in the Red Book for decades, many novice collectors have found machine doubling and thought they had just found the super-rare doubled die. One easy way to spot the difference is that most machine doubling that involves the date will also show on the mintmark, but because the date was hubbed into the dies and the mintmark punched in at a later time, the true 1969-S doubled die will not show doubling on the mintmark.

Extreme die polishing tends to show on more coins this year than in years past, sometimes removing part or all of some device edges such as the vest edge, throat, and neck. These are rather common and warrant no premium value other than as a conversation piece.

RPMs are widely scattered this year and many of them are minor. These are two of the better ones. On the left is 1969D-1MM-002 and on the right, 1969S-1MM-003. Photos by author.

Machine doubling, or strike doubling, is quite common this year. Notice that the outline of LIBERTY around the doubling on this cent is the same width as the normal devices on other coins. This is one of the hints that this is not a doubled die. Photo by Bob Piazza.

1970

Mintage of 1970 cents dropped somewhat from 1969 levels. However rolls and bags are more numerous and thus easier to find. San Francisco production increased (the only facility that did so), but it was at a cost. The most valuable yet most difficult to detect small and large date varieties were used at the San Francisco Mint this year in both proof and business strikes. To date, no examples of small date cents have been found or reported for either of the other two facilities, and given that we are currently over 30 years past 1970, none will likely ever be found. Slight variations in date size due to the age of hubs and dies for 1970 plain and D mint cents have been touted as "medium" and "large" date cents, but these are the result of polished dies or late die state coins, and are not an actual design change.

Small date 1970-S cents can be detected from the large date 1970-S cents, although doing so has always been a challenge. Although some still try comparing the digits of the date to one another, many have gone to looking at the strength of LIBERTY as it was hubbed into the die. Small date cents almost always have a very weak LIBERTY with the BER nearly completely gone. This characteristic also exists on some of the large date cents, and although to a much lesser degree, it can still be indecisive enough to warrant it being a less than perfect pick up point.

The one difference that exists between all 1970-S small and large date cents, and does not take a side-by-side comparison to detect, is in the seven digit of the date. ALL 1970-S large date cents (proof and business strike cents) have a horizontal crease running across the bottom of the horizontal bar separating it from the lower diagonal bar. NONE of the 1970-S small date cents will exhibit this crease.

Doubled dies are quite numerous for 1970, many of them having to do with the date and the L of LIBERTY. A large number of different dies has been found to date, and new ones are being added on a regular basis. Proof cents also exhibit a number of nice doubled dies this year, including a small over large date hubbing and a tripled die obverse.

One 1970-S doubled die deserves special mention because it is one of the nicest, yet most elusive, Lincoln cent doubled dies known. Its spread is much like that of its predecessor, the 1969-S doubled die. However, it is even more rare. Fewer than two-dozen examples are known to exist, many of which are uncirculated and have been known to sell for over $20,000. Although there is nothing to support the claim, I believe there are more copies of this doubled die out there in bags or rolls waiting to be found by a lucky hunter.

Repunched mintmarks are quite limited, just like those of 1969. One very nice RPM exists on 1970-S cents and is typically found in mint sets, but this one single case is about all there is to say for the year. Given the higher mintage than in the wheat cent years and the fact that there are fewer than two-dozen different dies known, the expanse between these dies in the sheer number of coins minted is great. Good luck finding them.

1970S-1DO-005 shows a nice counterclockwise spread from a very weak hubbing of the 70. On later die state specimens the only part of the doubling that shows well is the lower part of the zero. Photo by author.

Small Date

- 19 of the date is usually slightly weak.

- 9 of date is wider and more sharply curved.

- LIBERTY is usually very weak.

- Top of numerals of the date are level.

- NO horizontal crease across the 7 numeral.

Large Date

- 19 of the date is generally strong.

- 9 of date is narrower and more gently curved.

- LIBERTY is usually about normal.

- Top of 7 is lower than 9 and 0.

- ALWAYS a horizontal crease across the 7 numeral.

1970S-1DO-002P shows nice tripling on all outer obverse devices. This tripled die is rather scarce and commands a nice premium. Photos by author.

1971

Although mintage increased somewhat in all but the San Francisco Mint this year, availability of 1971 cents seems to be limited. Uncirculated bags and rolls do exist, but they are becoming rather difficult to locate and expensive compared to surrounding years. Quality of 1971 cents in general is also somewhat questionable. A number of coins plucked from rolls tend to be spotty and lacking luster, probably because of poor storage.

Doubled dies are plentiful in number again this year, and for a few lucky proof set hunters, very profitable. Two very nice class 2 doubled dies are known for the 1971 proof cent that, when found, turn a set purchased for a few dollars into one worth thousands. Other very nice doubled dies are known for 1971 on Philadelphia minted cents. Denver cents sport a number of doubled dies, but all known examples are rather minor.

Repunched mintmarks are rather few and far between this year. Some of them are quite nice, but all are difficult to locate and are at least somewhat more valuable than in surrounding years. Sales and auctions for 1971 RPMs tend to be as widely scattered as finding the coins. I noticed fewer than one dozen online auctions of legitimate 1971 RPMs during 2003.

Cents from this year also tend to show a lot of die fatigue, die scratches, die clashes, and machine doubling. Under the microscope, a number of them look horrendous. Because of the fatigue and die polishing, many of them will feature nearly missing or missing edges to some of the design elements and devices. One such example is called a "floating roof" cent on which the edges of the lower half of the memorial building's roof were removed by polishing

A "floating roof" cent shows die polish marks where an abrasive polishing completely removed the line that separates the edge of the roof from the field. Coin by R. W. Frye, photo by author.

the die excessively. This gave the upper half of the roof the appearance that it was floating in mid-air. These whimsical pieces were at one time cataloged and given value based on thin air, and that market (if there ever really was one) has since collapsed. Although some collectors still seek these pieces, the general majority of collectors have moved on. All one should expect for these mere conversation pieces is a dollar or two.

While the cherries are out there for this year, a lot of patience will be required to locate them. Dozens of rolls, if not over a hundred, may be required to find one nice die variety.

1971D-1MM-002 is one of the nicer RPMs one can find on this year's cents. Notice how neither mintmark can be called the "primary" mintmark because parts of each of them overlap the other. This kind of spread is called "tilted." Photo by author.

1971P-1DO-001 shows a very strong example of class 2 distorted hub doubling. Notice that the spread is toward the edge of the design on all outer devices. This doubled die is scarce and commands a nice premium, especially in uncirculated grades. Photos by Bob Piazza.

1972

For the first time since 1949 the Philadelphia Mint recorded more cents produced than the Denver Mint, mostly due to cent shortages in the East. Denver and San Francisco mintage dropped somewhat, but not enough to affect the current value of the coins. Rolls and bags from all three mints can be found, although original bank wrapped rolls and sewn bags are becoming scarce.

The production increase in Philadelphia meant taking shortcuts, and that came at a cost to the quality of the coins minted. Some time around the middle of this year, the discovery of a new doubled die cent caused the whole numismatic community and a large part of the general public to sit up and take notice. Unlike the 1955 doubled die that started the die variety craze, the 1972 doubled die gained immediate fame and was in the mainstream news across the country. Thousands rushed to the banks to get new rolls of the coins to look for these treasures that were already bringing $100 per coin in the numismatic marketplace.

It wasn't until later in the year that it was discovered that there were weaker and stronger doubled dies. In fact, quite some time later there came to be nine different recognized doubled dies for the Philadelphia minted cents and six different doubled dies for the Denver minted cents. Some stories circulated that a hubbing press operator filed off the fitting keys from the dies in order to get his job done faster, thus creating all these doubled dies. While I cannot confirm the story, the assumption is that something like this must have occurred. The doubled dies created this year are numerous, and many of them are nice.

Not to be missed or overlooked are a handful of different doubled dies on 1972-S cents as well. While the 1972-S business strike and proof doubled dies are far less advertised than their Philadelphia and Denver Mint counterparts, they are still collectible and hold value of their own.

Master die doubling occurs again this year and has fooled many people because of it having been listed as a doubled die by a number of entities. Although nicer than the doubling of some of the doubled dies listed within this book, the master die doubling of 1972 exists on nearly half of all coins minted for the year to include all three operating mints and the proof coinage. For this reason, it carries no premium value at all and should be disregarded as a doubled die. Master die doubling is too common to be collectible as anything other than a "normal" coin.

Repunched mintmarks are limited this year, and many of them are minor. Controversy exists over whether a number of coins with what appears to be a minor RPM are actually RPMs or mintmark punch damage. It is my opinion that these are genuine RPMs and are being listed as such by coppercoins.com. Because they are controversial, the ultimate decision as to their collectibility will be left to the collector.

While many of the 1972 rolls and bags have at least been searched through for the major die varieties, a number of the more minor die varieties are still out there waiting to be found. Although not nearly as valuable as the famous dies for the year, these more minor gems can bring upward from $10 per coin, so searching for them is well worth the effort.

1972P-1DO-009 shows doubling only above the 2 of the date and is commonly missed. In addition, a number of 1972 cents have a very small amount of doubling in this area that is mistaken for this die. Photo by author.

No Lincoln cent book would be complete without showing photos of the most famous doubled die of the memorial era. This is 1972P-1DO-001, a major doubled die that sells for well over $500 in GEM uncirculated grades. Photos by Bob Piazza.

These photos show the master die doubling that is very common to 1972 cents. This is commonly referred to as "die 5" master die doubling because of its listing in old references as the fifth different doubled die known, but has since been moved to master die doubling status. These are commonly offered for sale as doubled dies, but as with any master die doubling, these are worthless as die varieties. The doubling is very minor and shows on various areas of the design. It shows to differing degrees depending on the condition of the die when it struck the coin. This particular example is a sharp early die state. Photos by author.

1973

Cent production increased this year over last year by over a billion coins, one of the largest jumps from one year to the next in cent history. Bags and rolls are very plentiful and sell at levels right around double face value for all three mints. Quality is about the same as for the past few years. Discolored, spotted coins and heavy die polishing tend to be the norm.

A new reverse master hub was created for use this year featuring designer's initials that were more than twice the size of the same feature in 1972. At the end of the year, this feature was moderated somewhat, making 1973 cents a one-year reverse design type. I have searched for more than 20 years looking for a mismatched reverse type and have not found a single example to date — surprising that the Mint was so thorough about something so small. Discovering a mismatch would still be worth the effort to flip them over and look anyway.

Doubled dies and repunched mintmarks are very widely scattered and very minor this year. The ones that are known are barely worth the effort to look for, but this should not discourage collectors from looking. There are still millions of 1973 cents that have never experienced a discerning eye with magnification.

The 3 digit in the year has an odd shape which is sometimes mistaken for a doubled die. The center of the numeral exhibits a split and the outside edge sometimes looks doubled, depending on the die state of the coin and the condition of the hub when the die was created. This is normal and should be disregarded. This is the only year of cents on which this particular 3 digit was used.

The normal shape of the 3 on a 1973 cent. The center point is often confused as a doubled die. Photo by author.

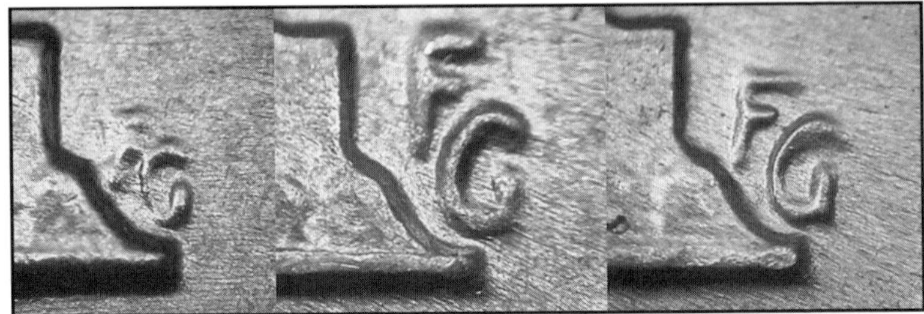

The initials on the reverse of the cent for 1972 (left), 1973 (center), and 1974 (right). Searching for mismatches of reverse types has been unsuccessful to date, but that does not mean they do not exist. Photos by author.

The date this brockage was produced would have been nearly impossible to tell if it had not been for the fact that 1973 is a one-year type. The initials on the reverse are clearly the 1973 style, which gives us the answer. Photos by Jeremy Katz.

1974

1974 was a problematic year for the Lincoln cent and the U.S. Mint. Copper prices rose through 1973 to a level that made cent manufacturing costs unprofitable. Different alloys were tested through the latter part of 1973 with little success. Aluminum was the best choice they had after testing copper plated steel without luck. Over 200,000 pieces were struck in aluminum and dated 1974 for the expected year of their release. Samples of the 1974 aluminum cents were passed around to legislators while lobbying for the change, but it was never to be. The samples were collected, the program scrapped, and all of the test coins were officially destroyed, although a quantity — believed to be six — escaped destruction. One of the surviving coins is in the archive of the Smithsonian.

Hoarding of cents was two-fold in reason. The elevated copper prices was one, but the other reason was that San Francisco minted cents were always in shorter supply than the other two mints because they typically minted only a third of the number of coins. In 1974, measures were taken to halt this hoarding by mixing the S mint coins with cents from the other two mints in unmarked bags. This did nothing to help the situation and in fact it exacerbated the problem. It was clear there was little the Mint could do to force S minted coins into circulation. Mostly for this reason, 1974 would be the last year of circulating S mint cents. The San Francisco Mint once again ceased regular coinage production in 1975, only minting dimes.

Both the obverse and reverse designs were changed this year as well. The reverse design's relief was slightly lowered and the exaggerated designer's initials were shrunk down to near their original size as designed in 1958. The obverse was initially redone in a more detailed fashion from the 1973 obverse then changed again to move the devices farther from the rim. This created two slightly different obverse designs for 1974.

Called either type 1 and type 2 or "large date" and "small date" respectively, the size of the date really did not change much. The best pick up point to use for the difference is in the clearance between the motto and the rim. The first design used, the large date, has very little clearance between the rim and letters of IN GOD WE TRUST, and has thicker, more blunt digits in the date. The small date design has more space between the motto and rim and has sharper, more pointed digits in the date. Both types were struck at all of the mints in business strike; however, all proof cents are large date.

The reason why the two different designs never gained much attention from the mainstream numismatic community is somewhat a mystery, though it likely involves two facts. First, the difference wasn't immediately noticed. Even though it is more widely publicized now, the difference is still difficult to detect without specific pick up point education. Second, reports claim that both designs are equally distributed, thus carry the same value, unlike the highly scarce and sought after 1970-S small date cents. I have found, however, that the S minted small date cents are considerably more difficult to find than their large date counterparts.

Yet another oddity with the Mint and their operations this year includes the fact that the West Point Mint in New York began striking cents this year. Because their facility was small and mintage would be quite low, the decision was made to leave the mintmark area blank so as to make the coins minted there indistinguishable from those minted in Philadelphia. Their plot was successful, as there is no way to distinguish them from Philadelphia minted cents.

Doubled dies are limited this year, as are repunched mintmarks. None of the known die varieties for this year are anything more than modest. However, large date cents have been reported as class 6 doubled dies due to confusion over the date size change, a general lack of knowledge of their existence, and their thicker dates. There are class 6 doubled dies for the large date variety, though some experience, patience, and good images to use as a guide will at first be necessary to discern the difference between the doubled dies and normal coins.

Rolls and bags of cents are easily obtainable for this year, and for good reason — they have never gained much value because they were hoarded more than they were used. It is still recommended to obtain a good roll set of all six varieties for the year and sock them away. Some day the general market may be in on our secret!

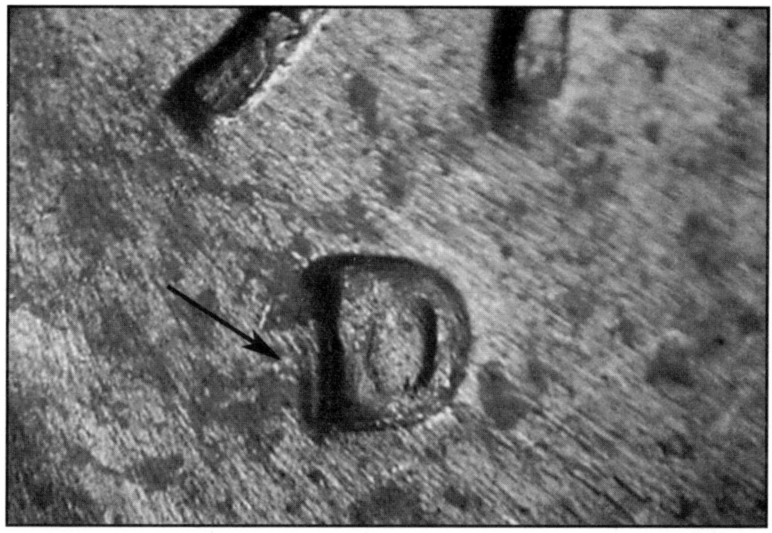

1974D-1MM-001 shows a rather nice separation to the west. This is not the only known RPM for 1974-D cents. Photo by author.

Although quite minor, 1974S-1MM-001 shows a very close north spread. Most proof RPMs are minor because the care taken inspecting them before use generally catches the die varieties. Photo by author.

1974D-1DO-001 shows a rather minor class 6 doubled die that shows generally in WE TRUST of the motto. Photos by author.

The 1974 large date (type 1) cent has noticeably thicker digits in the date with a rounded point on the 7, and very little clearance between the motto and the rim. Photos by author.

The 1974 small date (type 2) cent has noticeably thinner digits in the date with a sharp point on the 7, and more clearance between the motto and the rim. Photos by author.

1975-1979

Production of cents was in high gear these five years. The Philadelphia and Denver Mints, with the help of the clandestine West Point Mint, produced no fewer than eight billion cents each year, topping it off in 1979 with the first ever occurrence of ten billion coins of the same denomination minted within a single year. With these extreme numbers of coins came die overuse and other problems such as overpolishing, die cracks, and die breaks. In as few words as possible, cents from these five years are shoddy in quality. Early die state, fully struck cents from any of these years that grade full MS-68 or higher would be extremely rare and valuable.

With quality problems come a lack of die varieties. If most of the coins are of very late die state and have very mushy details, hub doubling becomes impossible to detect, if in fact it ever did exist on the die. Fewer than a half dozen known doubled dies exist during this period, and all those are on 1975 and 1976 cents. Because the only mintmark used at this time was in Denver, and because that mintmark was little more than an insignificant dot, repunched mintmarks are also nearly non-existent. Only two repunched mintmarks are known for 1979-D cents, and none for the other four years in this period. In fact, 1977 and 1978 represent the first two years together in the Lincoln cent series with no known die varieties.

One variety well worth mentioning is that the S mint proof cents of 1979 exhibit two different mintmarks. The standard mintmark that had been used since the San Francisco Mint reopened was replaced late in 1979 with a thinner, clearer version. Collectors dubbed the first mintmark style used in 1979 the "type 1" or "filled S" variety, and the second style the "type 2" or "clear S" variety. Without question the clear S variety is both far scarcer and more valuable.

The corner broke off of a mintmark punch in 1979, causing many 1979-D cents to have a split lower serif. This is not a repunched mintmark and should be disregarded.

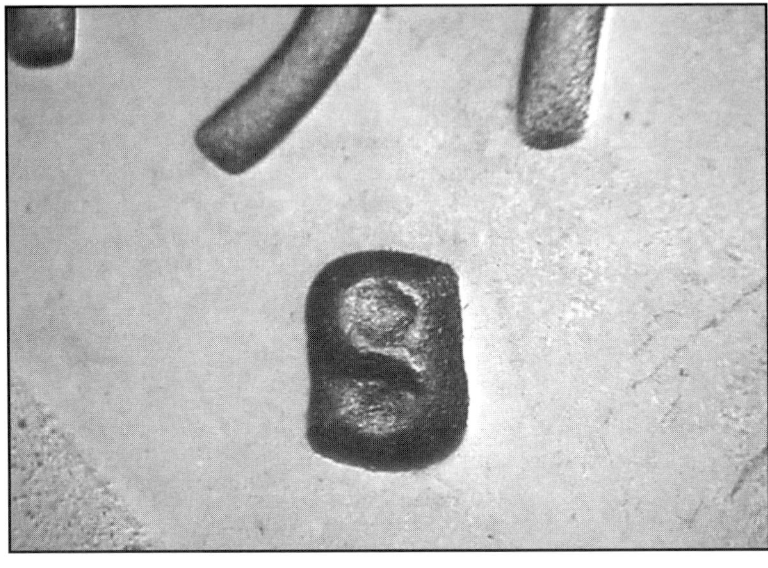

It is rather easy to separate the difference between the worn out and indistinguishable 1979-S type 1 mintmark (above) and the much clearer type 2 mintmark (below). Do not be confused, the type 2 for this year is the same as the type 1 for 1981-S.

1980-1981

The Mint found their critical mass in the quantity of coins they could mint these two years. Over twelve billion cents were minted in each of these two years — enough for three coins for every man, woman, and child on the planet with more to spare. Although more were minted in certain years to follow, the twelve billion per year mark is on the high end of what the Mint has produced each year since 1981.

Given these facts, it is understandable that even today there are more bags and rolls of 1980 and 1981 cents on the market than it can bear. Rolls sell for around double face value, and bags sell for less because the trouble of carrying them around is worth some discount. At best, selling rolls and bags of 1980 and 1981 cents is difficult, and nearly impossible over the Internet, because shipping them costs more than the coins are worth.

The good news, however, is that 1980 sports one really nice doubled die and a very interesting OMM! The doubled die has a very strong rotated spread showing on all devices including the date, and typically sells for $25-$50 in uncirculated grades.

The OMM is a very odd occurrence given the fact that the S mintmark had not been used on business strike cents for 6 years. How an S mintmark found its way onto a D mint die is a bit of a mystery, although it must be remembered that the S mintmark was still being used on proof issues. Although nearly a half dozen different possible OMMs were reported by the printing of the first edition of The RPM Book in 1983, only one stood the eventual test of time after being deleted from, and then reinstated to listing systems over a period of 15 years.

Like with 1979 proof cents, 1981 proof cents also bear two different mintmark styles. The second style of 1979 survived through 1980 and most of the way through 1981 production when it had to be changed. The new mintmark style is somewhat thinner and clearer and is much more difficult to differentiate from the earlier style than the 1979 versions. To keep with tradition, the first style used this year is called the "filled S" or "type 1", and the second is called "clear S" or "type 2." This has caused some confusion because the style used as the "type 2" for 1979 matches that of "type 1" for 1981. The type 2 mintmark style for 1981 is far scarcer than the type 1 and is also far more valuable. Take care in attributing them, as many people have been confused by their similarity and have purchased the type 1 for the much higher type 2 price.

On the left is the 1981-S type 1, or "filled S" mintmark, and on the right is the 1981-S type 2, or the "clear S" mintmark. The two main distinguishing features that can usually be separated without having the coins side by side is the open, perfectly round upper inside area of the clear S and the overextended and rounded upper serif on the clear S. Photos by author.

1980D-1OM-001, listed by Billy Crawford as 1980D COMM-001 shows evidence of an S to the northeast of the D mintmark. Photo by Billy Crawford.

These photos of 1980P-1DO-001 clearly show doubling in LIBERTY and the date. This doubled die is very scarce and brings a nice premium value. Photos by Billy Crawford.

1982

Enter the year where collecting memorial cents becomes much more interesting. 1982 saw a number of changes, not the least of which was a metallic composition change and a design modification. In addition, the Philadelphia Mint shattered the record for the most coins of a single denomination struck in one year by a single facility, with over ten billion cents minted. Like with the past two years, however, quality tends to be on the low side of expectations. Many very late die state coins with heavy polishing, die clash marks, die cracks, breaks, CUDs, and machine doubling do exist.

Late in 1981, the Mint authorized a change of the copper-based brass alloy of the Lincoln cent to a zinc core plated with a thin coating of pure copper in an effort to save money. Copper had become too expensive to use as the base metal for cents. Contracts were awarded to create the planchets for these new coins outside the Mint. The new zinc cents minted with these new planchets began surfacing in September, 1982.

During the same period that the change between metals was taking place, the Mint decided to modify the aging 1974 design of the cent as well. It is believed that the change to a new, lower relief design was to aid in striking the new zinc cents, but this is unconfirmed. The change in design created what would be known as large date and small date designs; the large date being the older design used first.

Because the change of metallic content and the change of design took place at relatively the same time, seven out of eight different possible combinations of the two were minted, with the only exception being small date brass cents from Denver (at least to date none have been reported!). Because so many coins were minted, none of the seven varieties are rare or even scarce. However, problems with forcing the copper to adhere properly to the zinc core and the horrid disfigured coins that often resulted make the zinc cents more desirable in uncirculated rolls. In fact, the least common of all seven varieties, the small date zinc cents from Philadelphia, now trade for over $2 per uncirculated coin and over $50 per uncirculated roll!

Two nice doubled die obverse cents are known for 1982 large date brass cents. Both are nice, but one is nice enough to warrant attention from generalist collectors, slightly elevating its value. Even though a slightly more clear and larger mintmark punch was used this year, only one repunched mintmark has been reported, and it is rather minor. The San Francisco Mint started using a new punch for proof cents this year as well - it has a pointed upper serif, which is reminiscent of those used in the 1940s and 1950s.

The D mint punch used this year chipped inside the vertical bar, leaving most of the cents for this year with a slightly disfigured mintmark. These are not repunched mintmarks; they are very common and warrant no premium value.

1982 cents are usually very difficult to find in a high grade matched set for a number of reasons. A general lack of quality of the worn large date design and the problem with the new zinc planchets saw many coins enter

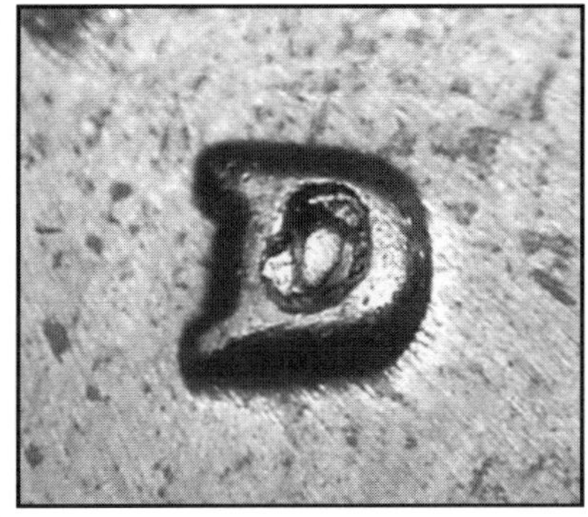

1982-D cents of all three types usually exhibit a broken mintmark punch as seen here. Do not confuse these for repunched mintmarks. Photo by author.

circulation at the hands of disgusted collectors and dealers trying to build acceptable rolls and date sets (because no mint sets were issued this year).

What's more, because of this lack of quality, many collectors opted to keep their sealed material (bags and rolls) intact because opening the sealed material could reveal less than desirable results. Much of this sealed material remains so today.

Finding the difference between the two metals can be done in a few different ways. First, weighing the coins will reveal quite a difference between them. The brass cents will be heavier (3.11 grams) than the zinc cents (2.5 grams), which are about 20 percent lighter.

The other popular method is to drop the coins from an inch or so above a wood surface and listen to the noise they make as they settle. A brass cent will make a high-pitched ring, while a zinc cent will have no ring, but more of a dead thud-like lead.

Yet another method involves looking at the surface texture of the coins. Gas bubbles were often trapped under the copper plating on zinc cents and will usually be evident to some degree, even if very minor. This phenomena does not happen on the solid alloy brass cents. Due to die wear, the flow lines are also different between the two metals, but this difference could take a lot of practice to distinguish. Brass cents typically have a more unevenly textured flow pattern.

1982P-1DO-001 shows a nice class 6 distended hub doubled die obverse. The spread is most notable in the motto. Photos by Bob Piazza.

1982P-1DO-002 shows nice doubling in the motto and LIBERTY, and very slight doubling on the 2 of the date. This doubled die is quite scarce, bringing over $50 when it is offered for sale. Photos by author.

The 1982 large date (above) is larger in size than the small date (small) as is evidenced by this exact-size comparison. In addition the 8 digit on the large date has nearly identical upper and lower loop size, while the small date's upper loop is much smaller. The 2 digit is also much different between the two coins. There are many other differences between the date sizes. The lettering on the small date is sharper and clearer, and the bust of Lincoln was completely re-engraved. These differences, however, are not quite as noticeable as the date itself. Photos by author.

1983

The second year for the new zinc cents was unimpressive. Only a small percentage of the coins that left the Mint were of quality to make MS-66 or higher grades. Most still suffered from the unfortunate disaster that plagued the 1982 zinc cents — streaked plating, bubbles under the plating, planchet flaws, and split plating that exposed the zinc to air.

Striking pressure is also an issue with most 1983 cents. In the area opposite the shoulder on the reverse the word STATES and the motto almost always struck up incomplete and soft. Because of the problems with the plating and strike, finding true high grade superlative GEM condition cents from 1983 is an extreme rarity.

This year's cents sport some really nice doubled die obverses and a huge doubled die reverse, among others. In all, nearly a dozen different nice doubled dies are known for this date, all of them on Philadelphia minted cents. Like with 1982, the mintmark punch used for Denver changed again this year and one minor repunched mintmark is known, although others are believed to exist through unconfirmed reports.

Gas bubbles on an early zinc cent. Photo by author.

A word of caution goes out to all who consider buying sealed 1983 cents. Because normal storage conditions that would not adversely affect cents of past years could be unacceptable for the early zinc years, anything purchased as "sealed" should be done with extreme caution. Blotching, heavy black carbon spotting, and corrosion of bare exposed zinc are the rule, not the exception. Without a doubt, nice uncirculated cents from these years will become a rarity probably sooner than most would expect.

1983P-1DR-001 shows fantastic doubling all over the reverse. Coin by Roger Anderson, photos by author.

1983P-1DO-001 shows nice class 5 doubling in LIBERTY and the motto. The date does not show doubling on this die because it is near the pivot point of the doubling. Photos by author.

1983P-1DO-005 shows class 6 distended hub doubling on the date, motto, and LIBERTY. This particular coin also shows many of the problems that plague early zinc cents, such as black carbon spotting and plating splitting on the outside of the letters of the motto. This coin will certainly not last through long term storage in its current condition. Photos by author.

1984

By the end of 1983, it was quite obvious, even to those not inclined to pay attention, that cents were having trouble. Stories ran in the newspaper across the country to dissuade people from thinking the white powder on their coins was poison. Since most did not even know about the composition change, an odd white powder on a "copper" cent was quite disarming. Little did they know that their new cents were already showing signs of what would be one of the most disastrous chapters in the history of the U.S. Mint.

The zinc cents were eroding quickly once the copper shell split open (usually during striking) and the zinc inside, having been exposed to typical environmental conditions, was turning to zinc oxide. This chemical composition is a powder and quickly falls out of the copper shell once it goes through its change. This further exposes the zinc core inside the shell and exacerbated the reaction by providing additional cavity area for moisture to build. What we end up with is a hollow copper core and corroded bits of white powder inside.

The most common area for corrosion to occur is around the mintmark. This part of the cent's design is vulnerable when struck, because the straight 90 degree angle of incision splits the fragile copper plating. Because corrosion occurred around the mintmark and left a hole of missing zinc on the coin, novice die variety hunters saw what appeared as an RPM or error. This is not the case. RPMs would look the same on 1984 cents as with any other year, with split or notched serifs and obvious extra mintmark punching. The only error on these coins is the Mint's decision to make cents with a vulnerable metal.

One very nice doubled die is known for Philadelphia minted cents this year — so nice, in fact, that it is widely sought after by generalists as well as specialists. It exhibits a very wide spread to the southwest on the ear and beard. These coins, dubbed "1984 doubled ear" cents, trade for well over $100 in uncirculated grades, and because of the problems with the early zinc cents, finding one (and preserving it) in true GEM condition is quite a rarity and worth far more. One other minor doubled die is known on P mint cents, and a couple of very minor repunched mintmarks are known as well. As with any cent from this era, preservation is the key after purchasing or finding examples of these die varieties.

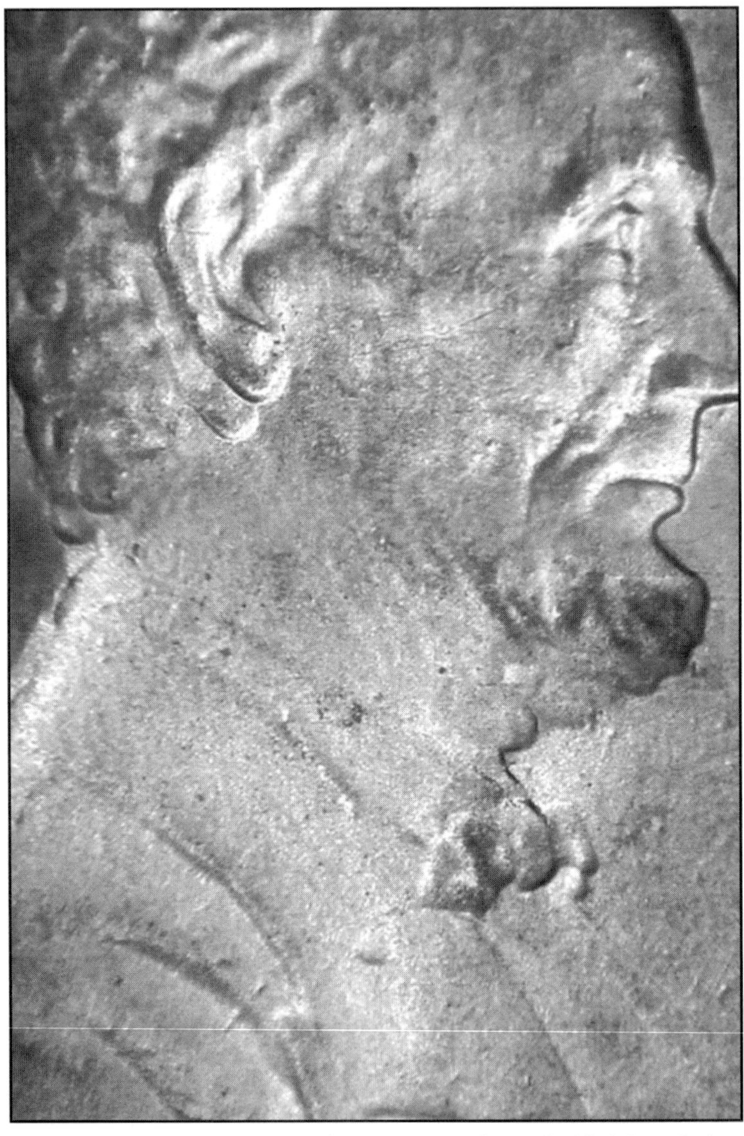

1984P-1DO-001 is one of the best known memorial cent doubled dies. It shows a strong class 4 spread on the ear, beard, and bowtie. This doubled die is rare and commands a hefty premium. Photo by Bob Piazza.

1985-1989

During the mid-1980s, the problem with zinc cents was slowly solved. 1985 and 1986 cents tend to show some problems, but most of these were solved by 1987. By 1989, cents were generally of good quality.

Before 1987, however, the horrid quality of zinc cents led many collectors to toss their coins back into circulation. This has caused a relative scarcity in these coins, and nice uncirculated rolls of 1984-1986 cents sell for far over face value. Prices reach a peak for 1986 rolls, which sell for over $20, (up from $9 just a few short years ago). I expects well-preserved rolls of 1986 cents from both mints to sell for well over $50 per roll within ten years (2015).

Doubled dies are hit or miss for this period, except in 1989, when there seemed to be a sudden increase in class 6 obverse doubled dies on Philadelphia minted cents, and in the more recently discovered class 2 and class 6 doubled die reverses on Denver minted cents. The other years in the group have produced some surprises, but they are very difficult to obtain in any grade. The class 6 obverses for 1989 number some half dozen dies altogether, and doubled die reverses for 1989-D cents are currently known for four different dies.

The Denver mintmark received another facelift in 1985, resulting in a much clearer and larger letter. The repunched mintmarks for these years are some of the most fantastic in the entire Lincoln cent series, but they, as well as the few known doubled dies for these years, are also quite difficult to find for three basic reasons.

First, there were a lot of coins minted these years — between four and five billion per year — resulting in a much larger number of dies used. This scatters examples of each different die farther apart, making any one of them more difficult to find. The analogy would be something like the older wheat cents being a bucket of sand compared to the current mintage figures being the whole beach.

The second reason is because a majority of the coins have already corroded, crumbled, and have since been tossed or destroyed. What may have been a half million examples of some die varieties could well be on their way to fewer than ten thousand remaining, and of those many are blotched or brown from circulation, have already corroded, or probably will.

Finally, cents are worth much less in commerce than they used to be. Increasing hoards of coins are ending up in pickle jars or coffee cans used as doorstops. One cannot find die varieties on coins that are not available. Offering to purchase such hoards may prove to be beneficial to collectors and to the hoarder — most do not want the coins, and are complacent about spending the time to roll them and cash them in at the bank.

On a final note, in 1985, the Mint began placing the mintmark for proof coinage directly on the master die. This ended the likelihood of producing repunched mintmarks and ended an era for die variety collectors.

Top Left: *1985D-1MM-002 shows a very nice south spread.*

Top Right: *1987D-1MM-012 shows a lightly punched RPM to the west.*

Below: *1988D-1MM-010 shows a nicely tilted RPM.*

all photos by author.

1987D-1DO-001 shows moderate class 2 + 6 doubling in the date and shows some minor doubling in TRUST. The remainder of the motto is shown here for marker purposes. Photos by author.

1989P-1DO-001 shows typical class 6 doubling for the date, most notable on this example in the date. Notice that the word LIBERTY gets thicker toward the center of the coin. This is in part due to the doubling, but also has to do with die wear. Often die wear can cause outer devices to appear thinner. Photos by author.

This example of 1989D-1DR-001 was submitted by Bill Slaughter. It shows light distorted hub doubling in AMERICA and on the lower extremities of ONE CENT. While not highly valuable, these doubled dies can be quite a challenge to find. Photos by author.

This 1989 cent suffers from problems that are common to 1982-1992 zinc cents. The spots seen on this cent are from a wash from the mint that did not rinse and dry properly. This coin came from the middle of a sealed roll and did not have exposure until unwrapped in this condition in 2002. The other problem evident on this coin is the raised ridge that shows going around two thirds of the edge of the design and greatly affects the motto. This is a late die state coin, and this is how the dies wear from striking zinc coins. This is quite unlike die wear one would expect to see on earlier cents. Photo by author.

1990-1993

With the copper plating solved by this time, the quality of cents from this period is greatly improved over those of past zinc years. Fully struck specimens, however, are somewhat difficult to locate until 1992, when a design change lowered the relief on Lincoln's shoulder allowing the STA of STATES to strike up more fully.

The obverse design change for 1992 also thickened the letters in LIBERTY and the motto, and at times have been confused for minor class 6 doubled dies. None of the 1992 cents reported to date exhibited hub doubling, but this certainly does not mean there are not any. Get used to the design by looking at a number of coins, and if any doubled dies surface, they should be relatively easy to distinguish.

One of the more noted changes in the reverse design of the cent takes place in 1993. The lettering was given longer, sharper serifs and was moved slightly closer together. This produced a reverse design where the A and M of AMERICA touched where they hadn't in the past. The earlier design used from 1988-1992 was kept for proof coin mintage. Three specimens have been reported to date where the design changed in 1993 was actually used to mint 1992 Denver cents. Therefore, it is believed that the new dies were produced in 1992, but were not intended to be used until 1993. These few examples of 1992-D cents with the 1993 reverse sell for hefty premiums.

1990 marks the year in which repunched mintmarks came to an end for business strike Lincoln cents. The Mint began placing the mintmark directly onto the master die, thus ending the tradition of hand punching mintmarks directly into each working die. This change had taken place on proof cents in 1985.

Doubled dies are all but non-existent in these years. A single 1990 doubled die obverse is known, a scattering of 1991 doubled dies are known for both obverse and reverse, and none are known at all for 1992 cents. One 1993 doubled die reverse shows a very weakly hubbed design to the northeast inside the memorial bays but nothing else.

Because of the improvement in quality more uncirculated rolls and bags were saved these years, resulting in lower values. Rolls and bags from

1990-1993 are readily available at double to triple face value, and typically contain very nice coins. Spotting and other problems seen in previous years' cents have been greatly reduced. However, ultimately the quality of these coins will depend on their storage.

Above: *The normal reverse used between 1988 and 1992 on business strike cents and from 1988 through today on proof strike cents. This is usually called the "type 2" or "wide AM" reverse. Photos by author.*

Below: *The reverse design used from 1993 to date on business strike cents. Notice that the A and M of AMERICA touch and the designer's initials are farther away from the base of the memorial. This is usually called the "type 1" or "close AM" reverse. Photos by author.*

1994

An increase in production this year was an effort to thwart a growing shortage of cents. The ever-growing opinion of the public was that cents were useless and worthless, and many coins ended up in jars, boxes, and other places other than in commerce. Another possible contributor to the shortage was that the cents minted during the 1980s were corroding away far faster than had been expected.

By most outward appearances, the 1994 cents appear to be roughly the same as in previous years, but die variety hunters know better. Two different doubled dies on the reverse of 1994 Philadelphia minted cents have caused the numismatic community to take notice. One of the two doubled dies shows an extra column hubbed between the far two right columns of the memorial building, and the other shows doubling into the steps on the memorial building. These doubled dies are quite scarce and command nice premium values.

The die that shows doubling in the steps of the memorial has been dubbed the "wavy steps" variety. Recently, these have been reported for other years' cents, to include those dating from 1993 to 2003, but oddly enough, all known specimens are on Philadelphia minted cents. Be attentive for them and you could get lucky.

This is 1994P-1DR-002, an example of the "wavy steps" doubled dies that have been surfacing on cents dating from around 1990 through 2004. These doubled dies are generally evident only in the single squeeze years of production but are known dating back to 1987. They are considered to be the first of a new classification of doubled dies. Listed as class 9, shifted hub doubling, they are caused when the die starts out of flush with the hub and snaps into place while the die is being pressed by the hub. Photo by author.

1994P-1DR-001 clearly shows doubling of additional memorial details inside the far right two bays and west of the left planter. Coin by Roger Anderson, photos by author.

1995

In March of this year reports surfaced that a doubled die had been discovered. Within another two months, coin periodicals were running advertisements for "1995 DDO" cents selling for upward of $150. Over a period of time and study, it became apparent that this doubled die had struck a full run of coins. This was determined by the number of different stage markers found on some of the coins. Since the doubled die had been found well into late die state, it was assumed that close to a million examples existed. This lowered the price of uncertified specimens to $10-$20, and certified specimens trade at $75-$100 only for high-grade coins, of which there are plenty. In fact, because the numismatic community so feverishly removed mass numbers of these doubled dies from bags, rolls, and circulation so early, there will likely be a plentiful supply of uncirculated specimens of this die decades from now.

What many do not know is that there exists a second doubled die on 1995 Philadelphia minted cents. Known as die number 2, this doubled die is more modestly spread and shows on all the obverse devices. While I have seen hundreds of the major doubled die offered for sale at auction and in shows, I have never seen an example of die number 2 offered.

The Denver Mint made its share of doubled dies this year as well. At least five different dies are known, one of them being really nice. 1995D-1DO-003 is a class 5 pivoted hub doubled die that was discovered by numismatic researcher and collector Gene Nichols in his pocket change in eastern Arkansas. In fact, many of the known examples of this die surfaced in the Mid-South. The other known dies for 1995-D cents are quite minor and command rather modest premium values.

Bags and rolls of 1995 cents have been affected by collector interest in the doubled dies. Rolls have been offered for widely varying prices from $2 through $10, and bags typically sell for $100-$200 if dated in February or March, the suspected time frame in which it is believed that the doubled die was minted.

The highly famed 1995P-1DO-001 is rather common yet still commands a nice premium value because it is so strong. It is estimated that nearly a million of this die variety exist. The key is to get a specimen that is in early die state. The coin photographed here is a late die state example, which is what most people are likely to get when they buy or find one. Photos by author.

1995D-1DO-003 shows strong class 5 pivoted hub doubling with a pivot point near 6 o'clock. Given this, the doubling only shows well in the motto and the details in the hair. Photos by Gene Nichols.

1996

Continuing the trend somewhat from last year, 1996 is best known for examples of close to a half-dozen different doubled die obverses. Although none of them are close to the big 1995 doubled die in spread, all of them are quite scarce and sell for nice premium values.

Rolls and bags of 1996 cents are readily available and are quite inexpensive, selling often for less than double face value to dealers and collectors. Quality is generally not an issue with these cents. Most freshly opened sealed rolls and bags contain a large number of very nicely struck coins with few spots or other problems.

1996P-1DO-001 shows light doubling in the date, VDB, and LIBERTY. These doubled dies are difficult to find because there are few dies known for the date and billions of coins to look through to find them. Photos by author.

1997-2004

This period begins the era of the "single squeeze" die making process. This method employs only a single hubbing of each die, thus eliminating the possibility of traditional doubled dies to a large degree. It has not, however, completely eliminated them. 1997 cents are closely watched by collectors for a doubled die that involves only the central area of the obverse, most notably the earlobe. Although this doubled die is hotly contested as being a mere die break by some, others agree that it is not a die break at all because the doubling also shows in the hair and inside the upper ear.

Other doubled dies that have recently surfaced have been the cause for a new classification of hub doubling. To understand this new classification, we must revisit the single squeeze hubbing method. In this method, a die is placed face up in the press. The hub is slowly pressed onto the die with increasing force as it smashes out the design incuse on the die. During this process, the die makes popping sounds as the metal flows and readjusts. If the hub is not perfectly flush with the surface of the die when the hubbing begins, it can slide into place during one of these pops, creating doubling on the die.

The new classification of hub doubling, class 9 shifted hub doubling, is currently not widely accepted, but is the only way to accurately describe the doubling on the resulting coins. Often, these coins show a shifted design with some degree of soft notching. However, they have not yet been known to show separation lines on the devices. This description alone eliminates all of the currently widely recognized classifications of hub doubling. Thus a new classification is in order.

Another anomaly that has been reported is the continued use of the design style abandoned in 1993 on the reverse of some 1998, 1999, and 2000 Philadelphia minted cents. Look for separation between the A and M of AMERICA, and watch for the positioning of the designer's initials, which are notably different between the two styles. These are somewhat common on 2000 cents, uncommon to scarce on 1998 cents, and very rare on 1999 cents. Each of these three oddities warrants premium values, and although they are listed in references, their value is determined more by market activity. The 2000 cents typically sell for $10-$20, the 1998 for $50-$100, and the 1999 for $200 or more.

Many people have reported these as being proof die reverses, but a close examination of over two dozen such coins has revealed absolutely no evidence that these coins were struck with a proof reverse die. They are simply the result of a pre-1993 reverse hub's continued use in die making.

Also during this period is the existence of yet another anomaly. In either 1996 or 1997, the Mint moved the placement of the mintmark from the master die (where it had been placed beginning in 1990) to the large plaster model used to create the master hub. They made both D and S mint plaster molds and used them in the creation of all master hubs. Those master hubs that were to be used to make Philadelphia master dies had the mintmark removed before creating the master dies. Some of the mintmarks were not removed completely, resulting in the appearance of a "ghost" or "phantom" mintmark on the coins. These have been reported and published for 1997 and 1998 coins, and I have found them on 1999 and 2000 coins as well, mostly in mint sets.

Just when collectors thought the die variety activity had ceased with the master hub mintmarks and single squeeze die making process, they continue to be pleasantly surprised with new oddities each year that merit attention. Though much of what collectors are finding and collecting in the most recent cents seems quite minor, remember that the Mint has gone to great measures to ensure these kinds of things would not happen and, for the better part, it has been successful.

This section would not be complete without mentioning that new discoveries are what make this hobby interesting. Researcher Billy Crawford is the discoverer of many of the newer doubled dies in the series, and to him I tip my hat for his dedication to the hobby and to his persistence in looking through what must have been a huge mound of coins to find a couple examples of what he insisted must still exist. Great going Billy!

1997P-1DO-001 shows what may appear to be a die break at the lower ear lobe, but it is actually a doubled die. This is evidenced in further doubling found in the hair and inside the upper ear. Photo by author.

Top: *A full shot of a 1997 cent with a phantom D mintmark. The area below the date clearly shows signs of a D mintmark. Photo by author.*

Bottom: *A 1999 cent that shows the same anomaly. Photo by author.*

Above: *2004P-1DR-001 shows very nice separation in the entire upper half of the design. Photos by Billy Crawford.*

Next Page: *2004D-1DR-001, discovered by Ron Howard, shows doubling to the south on the floor of the memorial building between the columns. Some doubling also shows on the side of the right planter. Photos by author.*

These two die varieties are clear evidence that hub doubling still happens today, even though the mint has tried to eliminate such things from happening with the single squeeze die making method. To date there are over two dozen different die varieties known on cents made in years since single squeeze became the only method employed for die manufacturing (1997).

9 | ADVICE TO COLLECTORS

I have but scratched the surface into what I believe to be one of the most fascinating, yet tedious hobbies I have ever encountered. To show you everything ever discovered and to completely cover the entire subject with a broad brush would take volumes to cover, which I do eventually intend to do. This, however, would still not include everything that's out there. It is believed that fewer than 50 percent of all the doubled dies and mintmark varieties in the Lincoln cent series have been found to date.

The best answer to the question, "What's in X year's cents?" can best be answered by showing you both valuable and insignificant attributes, and then letting you find the individual dies for yourself. If you learn what types of attributes to look for in a valuable coin, you will be better equipped to hunt through your coins. As the old saying goes, "Give a man a fish and you feed him for a day. Teach a man to fish and he can eat for a lifetime."

Identifying each different die can be a real challenge, especially without a good guide. My intent with www.coppercoins.com is to give you, the collector, the best possible attribution guide available with complete explanations and marker photos. This book, although packed with information, could not cover the scope required to successfully attribute dies and remain within one volume.

Have patience as you search through your coins. Get to know them and their design elements. The more you know your subject, the more you will know when that subject is anomalous. Instead of using a guide to find the coins, search through the coins, find the oddities, and then use the guide to identify them. Your efforts will be more fruitful, and you will be pleasantly surprised when you find that you have discovered something new.

Have fun with the hobby - enjoy it for what it is. Do not dig into a bag of coins expecting to pull out hundreds of valuable die varieties. Part of the fun of this hobby is in the thrill of the hunt and the satisfaction and reward you feel when you find a valuable coin, fully realizing the countless number of coins you had to look through to find that one true gem. Expect to have to go through a lot of coins to assemble a collection, and you will be much better prepared for your hunt.

I have spent nearly 25 years looking for the elusive doubled dies and repunched mintmarks. In that time, I have found countless valuable varieties. But there are still a number of them I have been searching for throughout that 25 years and still have not found. I know, however, that with patience, a fun attitude, and a little luck, anyone can be rewarded with countless hours of fun *Looking Through Lincoln Cents*.

- Charles D Daughtrey

the author.

FUTURE PROJECTS

I believe that collectors should have more power over their own collection, and in order to do that they need the tools to identify die varieties on their own. What is needed is a complete attribution guide. The only problem is that printing one in book form would consist of thousands of pages and several volumes.

A solution has been planned that will involve printing this information in periodical style packets that collectors can assemble into a book themselves. These packets will be hole punched for a 3-ring binder so the collector can choose a cover of their own in which to assemble their book.

Production of this book will begin in the Winter of 2004, and will run approximately four years. It will include articles, pricing information, new finds, and a number of attribution pages containing photographs, die attribute information, and marker information for every Lincoln cent die variety known.

The packets will be sold and distributed on a subscription basis and advertising will be available to help off set expenses.

For complete list of details on how to subscribe to or advertise in this exciting project, please contact the author's web site at www.coppercoins.com.

ATTRIBUTION INSTRUCTIONS

Coppercoins.com is now accepting public attributions of Lincoln cents. The following terms apply to anyone wishing to have coins attributed to the USCV (coppercoins.com) public die variety system.

Submissions must include no more than 12 coins unless prior and special authorization to send more coins in a single submission is granted.

IMPORTANT

Include a complete inventory of packaged items with your submission. Include the date, mint, and grade of each coin, along with a detailed explanation of what you see on the coin that warrants attribution. Also include (neatly printed or typed) your mailing address and your e-mail address on the inventory. If an inventory is not sent with the coins, the coins will not be attributed, and will be sent back to the owner at their expense. This is to cut down on time spent guessing why a coin was sent, and gives us a complete inventory of the contents of the package for repackaging.

A shipping and handling fee will apply to each submission received. This pays for packaging materials, postage, and insurance. ALL packages mailed out from our office will AT A MINIMUM be insured. Delivery confirmation or registered mail is optional at the submitters expense at exact postal service charges in addition to the basic shipping and handling fee.

A per-coin attribution fee is to be sent in addition to the shipping and handling with each submission.

Submissions accepted and sent via USPS (United States Postal Service) ONLY. No submissions will be accepted through United Parcel Service (UPS), or Federal Express (Fedex), and none will be sent via these or any other method either.

All attribution submissions are accepted on a first-come first-served basis. Credit for new finds or for existing listed die varieties for which photos are needed for the site will be given to the first submitter of said die variety in that die state. If a later submission is better in grade and warrants a retake of the photos, credit for the coin photographed will change to the new submitter. This is because coppercoins.com always wants to encourage those who have the highest quality coins to submit those coins for photography so we can continue to provide the highest quality die identification service to the public.

Submissions mailed to coppercoins.com become the responsibility of coppercoins.com upon receipt of the package, and this responsibility transfers back to the postal system when the package is mailed back out. We are not responsible for lost mail.

Coppercoins.com, upon receipt of each package, will contact the submitter to let them know the package has arrived, and will send an additional correspondence when the coins are attributed, and a final correspondence when the package is shipped out.

E-mail first to ensure my current turn around time for submissions is suitable for you before mailing them - cd@coppercoins.com.

Check for current attribution and shipping rates at http://www.coppercoins.com/attribution.php or by sending an email to cd@coppercoins.com.

Mailing address for correspondence and packages is:

C. Daughtrey
P.O. Box 6103
Springfield, MO 65801

Each package will be handled with the utmost care. References made available upon request.

GLOSSARY OF TERMS

abraded die doubling - caused by extremely worn dies (usually a working die) and appears as raised shadows of metal on the outer edges of the design. On the obverse it will generally affect the last digit in the date, the motto, and the first few letters of LIBERTY. On the reverse it will generally affect the outer edges of the wheat stalks and the motto.

annealing - the act of heating dies to strengthen them. Dies were annealed between each step in hubbing the design into the die.

bar-L - hub doubling that usually exhibits doubling only on the L of LIBERTY on Lincoln cents.

brass cent - any cent made between mid-1962 and mid-1982 with a composition of 95 percent copper and 5 percent zinc.

bronze cent - any cent minted between mid-1864 and mid-1962 with the exception of 1943 that has a composition of 95 percent copper and 5 percent tin and zinc.

bust - on the Lincoln cent, the portrait of Abraham Lincoln on the obverse of the coin.

CUD - a coin minted with a die that has a piece broken out of it. They will appear as "raised" metal near the edge of the design where the missing piece of the working die fails to strike the coin.

design - the collection and arrangement of devices on a side of a coin.

design hub doubling - a classification of doubled die (class 3) caused by hubbing different designs into a single die.

device - an element of a design on a coin such as letters, numbers, or pictures.

die - see master die and working die.

die break - a large die chip, usually completely filling a recessed area of the design on the coin.

die chip - a small missing piece of the die, usually in or around devices, that results in what appears to be extra metal in the void where the chip fell out.

die clash - the occurrence of two dies coming together without a planchet between them that results in transfer of the designs on the dies to one another.

die crack - the result of a crack in a die usually caused by age and pressure. On a coin it appears as a raised, jagged line that generally starts near a stress point and follows the path of least resistance — usually along the edges of devices.

die deterioration doubling - see abraded die doubling.

die error - damage that occurs to a die after it is placed into use on the coining press. Die errors transfer to the coins minted with the die at fault. Examples include CUD, broken die, and die clashes.

die gouge - a cut or nick in a die that results in a raised area, usually small, on the coins made by that die.

die scratch - small raised lines on the coin that are a result of abrasive cleaning of dies.

die variety - an anomaly in the design on a die caused by the hubbing press or by hand punching devices onto the die. Include doubled dies, repunched dates and mintmarks, and over dates and mintmarks.

distended hub doubling - a classification of doubled die (class 6) resulting from use of a hub that has flattened design elements which are thicker than normal. The effect on the coin is outer devices that spread toward the edge of the design usually without clear separation in the doubling.

distorted hub doubling - a classification of doubled die (class 2) resulting from use of a hub on a die that has been warped out of shape. The effect on the coin is outer devices that spread toward the center or edge of the design with separation lines in the doubling.

doubled die - used to refer to coins minted with a working die exhibiting hub doubling.

doubled eye (or doubled eyelid) - a form of hub doubling that causes all or part of Lincoln's eye to exhibit doubling. Usually caused by class 4, offset hub doubling.

early die state - describes a coin minted with a die that shows very little to no wear.

edge - the surface of a coin that connects the obverse to the reverse. It is the part that touches a surface when the coin is rolled on its side.

error - an anomaly on a coin caused by either the planchet making process or the striking process. They can happen as the result of a malfunction of the coining press or a working die that has faults caused by the striking process.

full strike - a coin showing complete detail.

galvano - a cast copy of the original plaster design for a coin coated in metal. Used as the original on the reduction lathe.

hub - see master hub and working hub.

hub doubling - the effect of hubbing a die on the hubbing press while the hub and die are not in proper alignment with one another

hubbing - the act of impressing a positive relief design into a die to create a negative relief working design.

hubbing press - a machine that uses a positive relief design (hub) with thousands of pounds of pressure to create negative impressions of that design into dies.

lamination - an error caused by an improper alloy mix used to make planchets for coining. The effect is loss of bonding between different layers of alloy that break apart before, during, or after minting the coin.

lamination peel - a separated piece of metal attached or detached from a coin as the result of lamination.

late die state - describes a coin minted by a die having moderate to heavy wear.

legend - On the Lincoln cent, "UNITED STATES OF AMERICA."

machine doubling - any doubling created on a coin by the striking process.

master die - a bar of hardened steel with the reverse impression of a coin design used to make working hubs.

master hub - the initial positive relief design used to create master dies.

memorial - refers to the entire building on the reverse of 1959-date cents.

mid-die state - describes a coin minted with a die showing minor to moderate wear.

mintmark - a letter or letters placed on a die minting coins used to determine where the coin was struck.

modified hub doubling - a classification of hub doubling (class 7) caused when either the design on a die is filled or the design on a hub is ground off to change one or more devices on the hub or die.

motto - on the Lincoln cent obverse, "IN GOD WE TRUST." On the reverse, "E PLURIBUS UNUM."

notching - a void in the corner of a device on a doubled die.

offset hub doubling - a classification of hub doubling (class 4) caused when a die is shifted in a cardinal direction between hubbings.

over date - a date punched into a die over a different date.

over mintmark - a mintmark punched over a mintmark with a different letter. Examples include an S over a D (S/D) or a D over an S (D/S).

pivoted hub doubling - a classification of doubled die (class 5) caused when a die is twisted between hubbings from a point near the edge of the design.

planchet - a coin blank with upset rims ready for the minting process.

planchet error - a defect on a planchet as a result of the planchet making process. Examples include clipped planchet, sintered planchet, and lamination.

reduction lathe - a machine used to reduce the design on a galvano to coining size. Creates a master hub.

repunched date - doubling of date digits as a result of hand punching the date, shifting the punch, then repunching the date.

repunched mintmark - a doubled effect caused by hand punching a mintmark onto a die, then repunching the same mintmark onto the die shifted from the original position.

rim - the raised border around the outside of the obverse or reverse of a coin.

rotated hub doubling - a classification of doubled die (class 1) caused by rotation either clockwise or counterclockwise of the die from a point near the center of the die between hubbings.

separation lines - the lines that run along the ridge of relief on devices that separate two sets of devices in doubling from one another.

serif - the overextended point of a letter.

spread - the distance of shift between two die hubbings or between two mintmark punches.

strike doubling - see machine doubling.

striking error - a defect on a coin as a result of the striking process. Examples include partial collar strike, broadstrike, and off-center coins.

tilted hub doubling - a classification of doubled die (class 8) caused when a die is not set flush in the hubbing press for a hubbing, then is set flush but rotated for a subsequent hubbing.

variety - a noticeable change in the design of a denomination of coin within a year; they are usually intended and usually minor.

very late die state - describes a coin minted with a die showing heavy to very heavy die wear.

weak strike - a coin not struck with enough force to show full detail. The highest points of relief will be flat. Very often mistaken for wear.

wheat ears or wheat stalks - the two devices on either side of the reverse of 1909-1958 Lincoln cents.

wheat grains - the design in the lower two thirds of the wheat stalks that look like grains of wheat.

wheat lines - the parallel lines near the top of the wheat stalks on the reverse of 1909-1958 Lincoln cents.

wheat stems - the 'sticks' on the bottom of the wheat stalks on the reverse of 1909-1958 Lincoln cents.

working die - a bar of hardened steel with the reverse impression of a coin design used to mint coins.

working hub - a bar of hardened steel with a positive relief coin design used to make working dies.

zinc cent - any cent minted after mid-1982 having a 100 percent zinc core with 100 percent copper plating.

BIBLIOGRAPHY

Allen, Brian and Wexler, John A. *The Complete Price Guide and Cross Reference to Lincoln Cent Mint Mark Varieties.* Stanton Publishing, Savannah, GA. 1999.

Fivas, Bill and Stanton, J.T. *The Cherrypickers' Guide to Rare Die Varieties.* Fourth Edition, Volume One. Stanton Publishing, Savannah, GA. 1997.

Flynn, Kevin and Wexler, John. *The Authoritative Reference on Lincoln Cents.* First Edition. KCK Press, Rancocas, NJ. 1996

Lange, David W. *The Complete Guide to Lincoln Cents.* Third Printing. Zyrus Press, Inc., Irvine, CA. 2005.

Taylor, Sol, Dr. "*The Standard Guide to the Lincoln Cent.*" Fourth Edition. KNI Publishers, Anaheim, CA. 1999.

Wiles, James Ph.D. *The RPM Book*, Second Edition: Lincoln Cents. Stanton Publishing, Savannah, GA. 1997.

Yeoman, R. S. Kenneth Bressett, ed. *A Guide Book to United States Coins.* 53rd Edition. New York, N.Y., 2000.

ABOUT THE AUTHOR . . .

Charles D. Daughtrey has been an ardent collector of the Lincoln cent since the early 1980s, and has been studying the die varieties of the Lincoln cent since 1985.

In his spare time while serving in Europe, he assembled an extensive collection of Lincoln cent die varieties, then added to that collection after returning from his tour of duty in 1990.

With the onset of the Internet, he immediately became interested in web development to show his artistic talent in an interactive format. In 1999, one of his first projects was an online study of the Lincoln cent, which eventually became coppercoins.com.

Chuck is a devoted father and husband. His son Michael and wife Evie are supportive of his effort to help other collectors with their numismatic goal, and his goal of completing a collection of Lincoln cents to pass on to Michael.

An independent web designer and developer, Chuck works and lives in his birthplace, Springfield, Missouri.

The Largest Book in

Have you ever wondered what it would be like to own the largest numismatic die variety reference ever produced? What would you say if you were told you could own that book for about 15 cents per day?

Enter the new era of die variety collecting and empower yourself to experience low-cost accurate self-attribution of your own collection. Instead of paying to have someone use the files to identify your coin, why not pay less and receive your own copy of the files? This book contains over 2,500 pages that are printed using high quality Hammermill® laser paper and the latest in HP Laserjet® technology, and it can be yours for less than a thin dime per page.

Every Lincoln cent die variety to ever cross the desks of author Charles D. Daughtrey and attributor Bob Piazza will be included in this book. Over 10,000 microscopic photographs, complete die marker information, cross-references to other systems, pricing and valuation information, educational articles, and a lot more right at your fingertips! This will indeed be the Lincoln cent book to have if you are even thinking about being a serious die variety hunter.

The system used in the coppercoins.com companion manual, "The Complete Guide to Lincoln Cent Die Varieties," is the United States Coin Variety system (USCV), the same system used in the book you are holding and on coppercoins.com and uscoinvarieties.com. It is the first fully public die variety system developed by collectors for collectors in that it is published in its entirety on the web.

Numismatic History...

The book will be issued in approximately 100-page packets as bi-monthly installments over a four year period at a subscription rate of $69.95 per year or $39.95 per six-month period. Expected date of release of the first packet will be January, 2005. To be placed on a mailing list for updates on the book's progress, email thebook@coppercoins.com.

Advertising in this book will be highly affordable, with ad rates as low as $11 per issue. Even collectors can get involved in having their contact information permanently placed in a book that will be a library mainstay for a number of collectors. Contact us for our inexpensive ad-rates at thebook@coppercoins. com.

This book is a real must-have for the serious numismatist or shop owner, and will not be mass-produced - ever. This is your opportunity. Take it. I guarantee you will be happy you did.

- Charles D. Daughtrey, author, owner...

The Only Web Resource for All U.S. Copper Coin Collectors.

With over a quarter century in the business, Springfield Rare Coin is a leading source for high grade rare coins in the Central United States. We take pride in our customer service and dedication to helping collectors and investors fill their numismatic needs.

We are located in Springfield, Missouri, but we deal nationwide and travel regularly to shows from Texas to Nebraska and Tennessee to Illinois. We will travel to buy or appraise collections or lots.

We deal in all series of United States coins in both collector and investor grades, certified or raw.

Give us a call or contact us by email and we will be glad to help you.

- Craig Warren, owner

email: spfldrarecoins@yahoo.com

206 N. Glenstone
Springfield, Mo 65802

(417)832-0669

fax: (417)862-3044